Encountering Correctional
Populations

Encountering Correctional Populations

A Practical Guide for Researchers

Kathleen A. Fox, Jodi Lane,
and Susan F. Turner

UNIVERSITY OF CALIFORNIA PRESS

University of California Press, one of the most distinguished university presses in the United States, enriches lives around the world by advancing scholarship in the humanities, social sciences, and natural sciences. Its activities are supported by the UC Press Foundation and by philanthropic contributions from individuals and institutions. For more information, visit www.ucpress.edu.

University of California Press
Oakland, California

Library of Congress Cataloging-in-Publication Data
Names: Fox, Kathleen A., author. | Lane, Jodi, 1967– author. | Turner, Susan, 1954– author.
Title: Encountering correctional populations : a practical guide for researchers / Kathleen A. Fox, Jodi Lane, and Susan F. Turner.
Description: Oakland, California : University of California Press, [2018] | Includes bibliographical references and index. |
Identifiers: LCCN 2017033397 (print) | LCCN 2017037977 (ebook) | ISBN 9780520966765 (ebook) | ISBN 9780520293564 (cloth : alk. paper) | ISBN 9780520293571 (pbk : alk. paper)
Subjects: LCSH: Criminology—Research—United States. | Corrections—Research—United States. | Criminal statistics—United States. | Correctional institutions—United States—Data processing.
Classification: LCC HV6024.5 (ebook) | LCC HV6024.5 .F69 2018 (print) | DDC 365.072/073—dc23
LC record available at https://lccn.loc.gov/2017033397

Manufactured in the United States of America

27 26 25 24 23 22 21 20 19 18
10 9 8 7 6 5 4 3 2 1

Kate's dedication:
To Chris, Jack, and Max Talbot

Jodi's dedication:
To Chris and Cooper Wilson

Susan's dedication:
To Stephen, Susie, and Tessa

CONTENTS

ILLUSTRATIONS

FIGURES

BOXES

ACKNOWLEDGMENTS

We thank Carrie Cook for providing insight about studying jail officers and Lora Levett for sharing her research assistant application. We also thank all of the people who have worked with us in the field over the years.

CHAPTER ONE

Introduction

PURPOSE OF THIS GUIDEBOOK

Over the years, the three of us have been actively involved in research with offenders and the people who attempt to control them through the correctional system. This means we often talk to offenders and others in the system and think about their lives. While many criminologists study offenders, offending, and its consequences, fewer actually journey into the correctional world. Indeed, this is not something that researchers are actively encouraged to do in some academic realms. Beyond our traditional doctoral studies, we received no formal training to prepare us for the exciting and challenging experiences associated with encountering correctional populations. Yet, along the way, we have learned for ourselves many valuable—and sometimes painful—lessons. Sometimes we learned them through trial and error, and other times we learned from researchers more experienced than we were. These are the kind of lessons that are generally absent from textbooks and graduate-level courses—the kind of lessons (or stories) that are often shared among scholars after hours over coffee or cocktails.

Our motivation for sharing these lessons in this book is to help equip people with the knowledge we have accumulated in our combined sixty-plus years of experience. We hope this book will encourage more people to do this kind of research by making it more approachable with fewer headaches. This book is particularly ideal for (1) scholars who are just beginning to conduct research with correctional populations, such as graduate students, faculty, and researchers, and (2) practitioners in correctional institutions interested in partnering with researchers to conduct research within their agencies or institutions. The book also is ideal as a supplemental text in graduate courses (e.g., general research methods, program evaluation, or corrections).

IMPORTANCE OF DOING RESEARCH WITH CORRECTIONAL POPULATIONS AND AGENCIES

For those interested in understanding offenders and reducing crime (e.g., politicians, academicians, and practitioners), studying the sources of the problem—the offenders and the ways we currently attempt to change their lives—often sounds logical and practical. Yet despite the massive correctional population, it can be extremely challenging (yet critically important) to access both offenders and the correctional agencies that monitor them. The following excerpt by John Hepburn (2013, 2) perfectly highlights what it is like to "get dirty" with original data collection with correctional populations:

Primary data collection requires that we leave the relatively sanitized and disinfected environment of the university and the clean routines of our offices to enter into the world of those we study. Through primary data collection, we glimpse the setting of our research, hear the sounds of the prisons, inhale the smells of the jails, observe the passing of rule violators and rule enforcers alike. We observe everyday activities, we "feel" the levels of tension, mistrust, and hostility, and we gain insights into the complexities of the relationships within the organization and among its personnel. We celebrate the fact that we emerge from the correctional agency or police department with both the data we sought and a greater knowledge and understanding of the working and living conditions of those we are studying.

So, *how* does one do this kind of research?

This book takes a practical "nuts and bolts" approach to explaining how to do research with correctional populations while recognizing that there are substantial differences across correctional facilities and populations. The approaches we use in various situations and encounters are by no means exhaustive of the many appropriate and successful routes to navigating research in the correctional world. Rather, they are examples of the lessons we have learned personally as we have navigated our research projects in correctional environments over the years. Moreover, following the advice we outline in this book will certainly not guarantee that readers experience the same outcomes, challenges, and enjoyment we have over the years. As readers undoubtedly have experienced firsthand already, the real world is riddled with infinite surprises. Working with correctional populations is like most things in life: it is an adventure best enjoyed along the way, not just at the finish line.

PREVALENCE OF PEOPLE UNDER
CORRECTIONAL CONTROL

A large number of people are under supervision within the correctional system, making this an important group of people for criminologists to study. At last count, nearly *seven million people* were incarcerated or under community supervision in the United States (Kaeble et al. 2015). Before talking about the nuts and bolts of doing field research in corrections, we discuss what statistics show about the different population groups that those interested in corrections might study.

Jails and the Jail Population

Jails incarcerate people in the "short term," meaning usually less than one year. Jails are often transient places because the average length of time people spend in jails is twenty-three days (Minton et al. 2015). There are approximately 3,000 local jails, a dozen federal jails, and 80 jails in Indian Country (Minton 2011). Jails incarcerate people who have been convicted of a crime and who are serving a short-term sentence as well as people who are not convicted (70 percent). Of the jail inmates who have been convicted, 22 percent are there for violent crime, 25 percent for property crime, 23 percent for drug crime, and 30 percent for public order offenses (Prison Policy Initiative 2016).

At last count, local jails in the United States admitted *12 million* people over the course of one year, with an average daily population of three quarters of a million people (Minton et al. 2015). Nearly another 10,000 American Indians and Alaskan Natives were incarcerated in jails in Indian Country (Minton 2011). The majority of local jail inmates are adults age eighteen or older (99 percent). The juvenile population (under eighteen years old) within adult jails is very small (1 percent) and has been significantly decreasing since 1999. Of the juveniles who are incarcerated in jails, most are held while charged as adults (84 percent). The majority of jail inmates are men (86 percent), although the number of women in jails has been increasing since 1999. In terms of race, jails incarcerate 47 percent whites, 34 percent blacks, 16 percent Hispanics, 1 percent American Indians, and 2 percent other races (Minton et al. 2015).

Prisons and the Prison Population

Prisons incarcerate people on more of a long-term basis, meaning typically longer than one year—and sometimes for a lifetime. The average amount of time prison inmates are incarcerated is 38.5 months (Adams et al. 2010). Prisons are operated by each state, the Federal Bureau of Prisons, the U.S. military, and private companies. There are 1,821 prisons in the United States, 23 percent of which are private. Most are state-run, with the remaining 6 percent federal (Stephan 2008).

As of the end of 2014, there were more than 1.5 million people incarcerated in state and federal prisons, mostly in public prisons (91 percent). Of the men in prison, 37 percent were black, 32 percent white, and 22 percent Hispanic. Imprisonment differs greatly based on race, with 2.7 percent of all black males, 1.1 percent of all Hispanic males, and 0.5 percent of all white males in prison. A similar pattern appears for race for women as for men. The number of people in prisons has been decreasing slightly each year since 2007, and the changes since that year resulted in an overall 0.3 percent decrease over the time period (Kaeble et al. 2015). Rates of imprisonment vary greatly by state, and they have also decreased over the last decade. At last known count, 54 percent of people in prison in 2014 were serving time for violent offenses, 19.3 percent for property offenses, 15.7 percent for drug offenses, and 11 percent for public order offenders (e.g., weapons law violations and driving under the influence). About 8 percent of state and federal prison inmates were veterans, of which 99 percent were male (Bronson, Carson, and Noonan 2015).

Parole and Probation Population

The probation population is the largest group of people under correctional control. At the end of 2014, about 70 percent of the people under correctional control were supervised in the community, meaning on probation (56 percent) or parole. Since 2007 the overall number of offenders supervised in the community decreased due to declining numbers on probation, despite the increase in the number of people on parole. In 2014, there were about 4.7 million supervised offenders in the community (Kaeble et al. 2015). People on probation (75 percent) and parole (88 percent) were more likely to be male. Comparing probation to parole, there were more whites (54 percent vs. 43 percent, respectively) than blacks (30 percent vs. 38 percent), Hispanics (14 percent vs. 17 percent) or others (2 percent for both groups). In terms of offenses, probationers and parolees committed violent offenses (19 percent vs. 29 percent), property offenses (29 percent vs. 22 percent), and drug crimes (25 percent vs. 32 percent) (Herberman and Bonczar 2014).

Juvenile Facilities and Population

Although jails and prisons often have more common characteristics generally in terms of structure and design, juvenile correctional facilities vary widely in design, style, size, staff, and program offerings. About 51 percent of facilities are public and the other 49 percent are operated by either nonprofit or for-profit organizations (about 12 percent are for-profit). As of 2012, there were about 2,547 juvenile facilities, housing 57,190 offenders under the age of twenty-one on the day of data collection.[1] Most of these youths are in placements that screen them for educational, substance abuse, and mental health needs (Sickmund and Puzzanchera 2014), which may be important sources of existing data for researchers.

Instead of "jail" or "prison," juvenile facilities are often collectively called "residential placement" and can include halls, detention centers, reception and diagnostic centers, shelters, group homes, ranches or wilderness camps, training schools, and residential treatment facilities (Hockenberry, Sickmund, and Sladky 2015). Juvenile institutions also vary in terms of their level of security. For example, while most lock youths in their rooms at least part of the day, often at night, a small percentage of institutions do not secure youths in the areas where they sleep, even at night. Moreover, while some facilities (about one-quarter) have security features that resemble adult correctional institutions (e.g., fences and razor wire), others do not even lock doors and have no fences (e.g., about 80 percent of group homes).

It is important to remember that, like adult offenders, more juvenile offenders (54 percent, in 2013) are sentenced to probation

---

1. Depending on the state, juvenile institutions can house youths beyond the age of 18, as long as they were sentenced as juveniles. For example, the upper age over which juvenile courts can maintain jurisdiction for disposition in California, Hawaii, New Jersey, and Tennessee is 24. In contrast, in seven states, 18 years of age is the upper limit. In Mississippi, the upper age is 19, and in 31 states and Washington, DC, the upper age is 20. Florida and Vermont allow juveniles to be held until 21 while Kansas puts the upper age at 22. Still a few other states allow jurisdiction to continue until the disposition is complete (Sickmund and Puzzanchera 2014).

than facilities (Hockenberry and Puzzanchera 2015). This means that focusing only on institutionalized youths ignores more than half of the juvenile correctional population. Although the Federal Office of Juvenile Justice and Delinquency Prevention (OJJDP) is currently funding the Census of Juvenile Probation Offices in order to learn more about juvenile probation, there is actually little current national information on probation officers, the numbers of juveniles on probation, or the particulars of their sentences (see OJJDP 2016). Still, these youths are an important group of juvenile correctional clients, and they—along with their supervising agencies and officers—can provide a rich source of information for researchers.

Correctional Officers

Nationally, jails employ nearly 200,000 correctional officers (n = 173,900), of which most are male (71 percent; Minton et al. 2015). The last known count shows that federal and state prisons employed 295,261 officers, 10,769 administrators, 51,993 clerical/maintenance staff, 11,526 educational workers, 46,016 professional/technical employees, and an additional 29,489 other (unidentified) employees (Stephan, 2008). Correctional officers are often exposed to stressful situations given job demands and the risk of victimization. A recent study found that 36 percent of prison correctional officers felt tense or anxious while at work, although the vast majority of officers reported feeling "generally pretty calm on their shift" (Steiner and Wooldredge 2015, 809). Jail staff face similar situations. Jail staff report that the danger they experience on the job is moderately high (Lambert et al. 2004). The daily shift for correctional officers and inmates is structured in large part by daily routines. For example, each jail and prison typically follows a predictable schedule with planned inmate counts, meals, recreation, religious services, counseling, and education services.[2] Of course, there also are a myriad of unplanned events that can and do arise in correctional institutions, including but not limited to physical altercations, injuries, shakedowns, and medical emergencies. Data collection and researcher's presence in jails must fit into the facility's planned and unplanned schedule of events because correctional institutions are highly structured environments that cannot easily change their daily routines to accommodate researchers. Yet, staff are often willing to make arrangements for researchers to collect data among inmates with minimal disruption to the typical daily events at the facility.

OUR EXPERIENCES CONDUCTING RESEARCH WITH CORRECTIONAL POPULATIONS

Before discussing the nuts and bolts of the lessons we have learned over the years, we thought it might be useful to give readers some background on our research endeavors that inform this work to provide some context regarding the tips we share.

Kathleen A. Fox is an associate professor at Arizona State University. Much of her research examines the victimization of offenders, especially among those who are incarcerated. She has personally interviewed prison inmates, read the details of prison inmates' crimes buried within their files, surveyed jail inmates across fourteen different jails, and examined the official records of

2. While many jails offer services for inmates, there are many challenges with service delivery in an institutional setting, especially one in which clients (inmates) are present for short periods of time. For example, programs and services in jails and prisons must have consistent agency and personnel support, strong evaluation designs, funding, and adequate time to execute (Tims and Leukfield 1992).

incarcerated juvenile gang members as they reentered their communities. She has lead teams of researchers and research assistants, received grant funding, gained access to correctional populations, and maintained positive relationships with correctional agencies. All of this occurred when she was an undergraduate student, doctoral student, and pretenure assistant professor at a Research I university. Her experience underscores the point that while collecting original data is very time consuming, it also can be compatible with (even complementary to) the constraints of one's other demanding career goals, including the race toward tenure.

Jodi Lane has been a professor at the University of Florida since 1999 and generally studies fear of crime and other attitudes toward the justice system and juvenile corrections. She has worked on two major grant-funded research projects studying juvenile correctional populations, as well as a number of other unfunded projects involving offenders and justice system personnel. Most recently, she was a principal investigator on an Office of Juvenile Justice and Delinquency Prevention (OJJDP) and Florida Department of Juvenile Justice (DJJ) project designed to evaluate the implementation of faith-based programming in juvenile correctional facilities (2004–2008). She also was a researcher on the RAND Corporation study of the South Oxnard Challenge Project in the late 1990s, using experimental methods to evaluate a multiagency approach to serving youth on probation. While in graduate school during the early to mid-1990s, she was a project researcher on the federally funded evaluation of the Orange County (California) Gang Incident Tracking System, working with twenty-two police agencies to collect gang data. In addition, she has supervised and collaborated with multiple graduate students on projects involving correctional populations and staff, especially those in jails, work release, and on probation and parole.

Susan Turner is a professor in the Department of Criminology, Law and Society at the University of California, Irvine (UCI). Trained as a social psychologist, she also serves as director of the Center for Evidence-Based Corrections. Turner worked at the RAND Corporation for over twenty years before she entered academia. Over her career, she has led a variety of research projects including studies on racial disparity, field experiments of private sector alternatives for serious juvenile offenders, work release, day fines, and a fourteen-site randomized design evaluation of intensive supervision probation with nearly two thousand offenders. Turner's areas of expertise include the design and implementation of randomized field experiments and research collaborations with state and local justice agencies. At UCI, she has assisted the California Department of Corrections and Rehabilitation in the development and validation of a risk assessment tool as well as evaluations of targeted parole programs. She is also involved with a number of organizations evaluating the impact of Arts in Corrections programs on correctional institutions and offenders.

HOW THIS GUIDEBOOK IS ORGANIZED

Following this introductory chapter, this book is organized into four substantive chapters. Chapter 2, "Gaining Access to and Building Rapport with Correctional Populations," presents tips for (a) identifying who grants access to correctional populations, (b) how to ask for permission to access correctional populations, (b) typical steps needed to obtain permission, (c) when to obtain access in conjunction with other research tasks, (d) convincing staff members to buy in to the research, (e) convincing the target population to participate, and (f) improving participation rates among offenders, correctional staff, and families of juvenile clients.

The third chapter, "The Types of Correctional Data That Can Be Collected," describes (a) existing major national data sources, (b) using existing correctional administrative data, (c) pros and cons of collecting your own data (e.g., surveys, interviews, focus groups, and observations), (d) program evaluation, (e) collaborating with agencies for hybrid data collection, (f) how to measure recidivism, and (g) data analysis skills needed for different types of data gathering.

The fourth chapter, "Informed Consent Process and Research Ethics," focuses on (a) institutional review board approval for different types of data gathering, (b) how to avoid harm to client participants, correctional staff, and researchers, (c) safety of the research team inside correctional facilities, (d) balancing participant benefits with researcher safety, (e) what to do if an inmate touches you, (f) what to do if you are accidentally locked inside a dorm alone with inmates, (g) safety when researching community samples, (h) how to avoid coercion of participants, (i) how to protect participants' identities, (j) parental consent/ assent: gaining permission and maintaining access to conduct research on juvenile correctional populations, (k) deception and disclosure, (e.g., ethics of deception, incomplete disclosure as an alternative to deception, and disclosing to participants other information related to the research), (l) ethics when reporting research findings, and (m) advice for applying for approval from university and correctional institutional review boards.

The fifth chapter, "Logistics of Doing Research with Correctional Populations," discusses general tips for conducting research with clients and staff, many of which cut across many correctional populations (probation and parole, juvenile facilities, jails, and prisons). Highlights of this chapter include: (a) preparing and training researchers to collect data from correctional populations, (b) appropriate attire for men and women, (c) questions to discuss with correctional staff prior to data collection, (d) what to do when offenders ask inappropriate questions or behave inappropriately, (e) education level and literacy of offenders, (f) accommodating offenders' education levels, (g) research with non-English-speaking participants, (h) correctional populations with special needs, (i) piloting the data collection instruments, (j) time-consuming setbacks and the importance of researcher flexibility, (k) importance of record keeping, (l) traveling to correctional facilities and populations, (m) where to conduct the research, and (n) other things to consider (e.g., minimizing exposure to communicable diseases, using the bathroom inside a correctional facility, making small talk, reporting unprofessional behavior, researchers coping with stress, and preventing participants from becoming distressed by the research). This chapter also contains special features on example interview questions for selecting research assistants, back translation and correctional settings, and researchers' gender, race/ethnicity, age, and sexuality.

Throughout this guidebook, we deliberately use the word *participant* where possible to refer to participating correctional populations (e.g., correctional staff or offenders). Where it is inappropriate to say *participant*, we use the word *offender* when speaking generally about a variety of correctional populations (e.g., inmates, probationers, parolees), particularly in chapters that pertain to all correctional populations. Other terms are used in places and chapters that focus on more specific types of correctional populations. For example, the word *inmate* is used when specifically discussing jail and prison inmates, *juvenile* is used to refer to children in juvenile facilities, and *probationers* and *parolees* are used to identify those under correctional control in the community. We realize that different groups may prefer different terminology in some cases, but we do not use these terms to imply value judgments. Rather, we use them so that the cadence of the manuscript can vary and be more interesting.

CHAPTER TWO

Gaining Access to and Building Rapport with Correctional Populations

One of the first steps in any research project designed to study the criminal justice system in the field is to gain access to the agencies, courts, institutions, and populations necessary to conduct the study. Because of the legal aspects related to the justice system, researchers generally must obtain special permissions to be able to collect data on people working in and managed by the system. For example, one cannot just walk into a criminal justice agency and observe the way one might in a public setting such as a shopping mall, restaurant, or recreation area. In addition, people who work in the system often must gain permission from their superiors before they can answer questions or allow researchers to enter their agencies and institutions to collect data. Gaining access to correctional populations, as we discuss in this chapter, takes a lot of planning and effort.

WHY ACCESS TO CORRECTIONAL
POPULATIONS IS OFTEN CHALLENGING

It is not unusual for correctional agencies to approach research-ers rather than vice versa, especially in terms of evaluation research. In recent years, this has been true because granting agencies often require an evaluation component as a require-ment for funding program delivery (Lane, Turner, and Flores 2004). Many correctional agencies do not have their own inter-nal research units and rely on outside researchers to help. How-ever, when researchers wish to initiate the partnership, they must navigate the process of gaining access to both correctional staff and populations. Prisoners are a protected research group to study, which often makes gaining access challenging (see chapter 4). Yet, there are other reasons why gaining access to correctional populations can be challenging.

First, *correctional agencies, or specifically their leadership*, may be leery of research. If agencies do not "need" research conducted for them, it may be tougher to convince them to allow outsiders inside their organizations. Many agency administrators gener-ally might have trouble allowing outside scrutiny of the daily activities in their workplace, but correctional agencies often have the added burden of worrying about the public and politi-cal ramifications if someone "exposes" something inside that is not ideal. If news agencies pick up stories about problems in cor-rectional institutions, leaders and staff may worry that the pub-licity will create bigger problems for them politically, with the public, and possibly even legally. This worry about exposure is a tough issue for researchers to manage. Even though the benefits of research should outweigh the risks, practitioners may still worry about what politically might happen if they give researchers too much access. In addition, program evaluations, in particular, can have the consequence of leading to the shutdown of programs if they show them to be ineffective, and leaders are often aware of this possibility (see Lane, Turner, and Flores 2004; Nyden and Wiewel 1992; Riger 2001). Consequently, it is very important that everyone involved in the project knows that study personnel are trustworthy. Of course, researchers have no control over decision makers regarding program delivery should decisions be made based on research findings to alter or discontinue a program, but researchers can be careful to assure administrators that their goal is to be objective and that they are not there with the expressed goal of harming the program and to follow through with these promises.

Second, *correctional staff members* may be leery of research. Individual correctional staff, whether in facilities or in community corrections agencies, may also fear that researchers are there to "expose" wrongdoing similar to an audit of their activity or similar to the way some investigative reporters might be. They also may be understandably nervous about telling someone about what they do or allowing themselves to be observed in action for fear of judgment. Consider what it is like to have even a peer come observe your own work (for example, ponder having an observer in the classroom taking notes on your own behavior and teaching style, especially over a period of time). It is hard to be comfortable and show one's typical self. Consequently, it is important for researchers not only to take the time to get to know the "real" people being studied, if possible, but also to consider the context of concern they experience. Two ways to manage concern, as we mention below, are to allow administrators who are in charge of approving the research and maybe even other staff members to put a few study items of interest in data collection instruments (such as surveys or interviews) and continue to assure them that answers are confidential and only aggregate data will be reported. We have found that spending time in correctional settings over time can considerably increase trust, because we are open, honest, and follow the tips we mention in this book. In addition, as people get used to having researchers around, they tend to become less guarded as long as they have productive or positive experiences.

Finally, *correctional clients* may also be leery of researchers, and their reasons for concern may be different than the worries that correctional workers have about the research. One of the biggest concerns of offenders, for example, is that system actors will punish them (probation or parole revoked or be arrested again, even inside facilities) if crimes unknown to the police are exposed. Remember that institutional review boards (IRBs) will not allow researchers to conduct research that could compromise participants, including make their lives more difficult under correctional control or harm their chances at parole. Simply, the risks of the research cannot outweigh the benefits for the people we study. Even so, scholars often ask offenders about their self-reported crime while on the street or their infractions inside the facility. Just being asked these questions can cause stress for the respondents and lead them to worry about the consequences of being honest on survey or interview questions, despite reading the informed consent. Even in situations where the researcher is not asking about crime, offenders may be suspicious of the researcher's motives or of what might happen with their responses. This is understandable, because many have been in positions of being judged for their behaviors or associations before, and they have a lot to lose if their personal information is shared—specifically, they may lose their freedom, either in the future or for a longer period of time. This is one of the primary reasons for ensuring we use standard IRB protections when conducting research and are extremely careful about ensuring these safeguards. Still, building and maintaining trust with both correctional staff and populations is of utmost importance.

In fact, building rapport is arguably one of the most important aspects of doing research with correctional staff and populations (see also Fox, Zambrana, and Lane 2011; Lane, Turner, and Flores 2004; Trulson, Marquart, and Mullings 2004). Researchers usually do not gain access to—or cooperation from—correctional populations without an *immense* amount of rapport building. This professional courtship among researchers, administrators, offenders, and correctional practitioners starts instantly—literally in the first *second* of meeting, people form lasting judgments about trustworthiness, competence, likability, aggressiveness, and attractiveness (Willis and Todorov 2006). And while first impressions with correctional administrators and participants are critical, it is also the long-term qualities that make for any successful partnership.

The following outlines specific tips for gaining access to correctional populations and building rapport with gatekeepers. While the discussion below will help researchers gain access and build rapport "from scratch," we wish to underscore the importance of seeking out help from senior colleagues—even those you do not know well—who may already have connections with the population of interest. Garcia (2016) suggests reading colleagues' vitas and requesting to meet over lunch or coffee to ask for help getting connected to gatekeepers. Other ways to meet practitioners and build partnerships as identified by Garcia (2016) include attending practitioner conferences, writing a blurb in practitioner publications about your research and how it can assist local practitioners, and volunteering to work on a small project for free to get one's foot in the door.

WHO GRANTS ACCESS TO CONDUCT RESEARCH AMONG CORRECTIONAL POPULATIONS

Gaining access to correctional populations can be one of the most challenging and time-consuming aspects of a research project. As noted earlier, sometimes correctional agencies initiate contact with researchers to partner. For example, we have had an ongoing partnership with the Florida Department of Juvenile Justice and had fostered relationships with this organization over many years, so the agency approached us first to create the partnership for a faith-based study. Yet, approval from the agency's own internal IRB was still necessary. Identifying who has the authority to approve research is among the first steps. We have also had longstanding relationships with many criminal justice and correctional agencies in California, which makes the initial startup of new projects easier than it might be otherwise.

Gaining Access to Prisons and Jails

Many prison systems have clear instructions outlining the necessary procedures for researchers who wish to request access to conduct research. This information may or may not be public, however. If a researcher is interested in conducting a study at a particular facility, it may help to start by contacting the leadership there. For example, in some prisons, the warden might be the first person to contact, and this person may designate a staff member to manage study details once permission is granted. Of course, there may be a number of "screeners" to talk to before gaining access to the warden (such as administrative assistants or assistant wardens). In other facilities, the warden may be the first contact, but the leaders at the state level may have the final say as to whether researchers may conduct the study. For example, years ago, one of our graduate students attempted to interview correctional officers and inmates about their experiences with informal social control in the prison. While the warden at a particular prison of interest was willing to participate, the state-level leaders denied the request, simply indicating that the study did not meet their needs. Even if access is granted, particular correctional systems may have their own IRBs for research, meaning that researchers will need to pass the study through both their own university IRBs and the department of corrections' IRBs.

If permission must be obtained at the state level (not at the local facility), there may be some information on websites to lead researchers in the right direction. For example, the Florida Department of Corrections website has contact information for their Bureau of Research Data and Analysis (e.g., http://www.dc.state.fl.us/orginfo/research.html). The California Department of Corrections and Rehabilitation also has a website that focuses on their research unit and initiatives (e.g., http://www.cdcr.ca.gov/Reports_Research/). But, neither of these sites contains much detailed information for outside researchers to consult when considering a new project. In other words, figuring out how to get permission is often trial and error. One must figure out how a particular system works in this regard—often by asking a lot of questions of people they contact—to determine with whom they should speak to gain the permission to proceed. It may take many phone calls, e-mails, and/or visits before the correct connection is made. It may be that obtaining permission at the state level means that access is granted to all the facilities of interest. But it may also be true that the state-level permission only allows researchers the permission to ask to do research and the details must be worked out with each particular prison.

In our experience, it is also challenging to identify the person who has the authority to approve research in jails. Jails are typically administered locally and may vary widely in organizational structure and procedures. Across fourteen jails in the state of Florida, we received approval to conduct research from captains, colonels, and/or majors. In other jails or local systems, researchers may need to request permission from people with even more administrative power, such as undersheriffs or the sheriff. Figuring out who can approve the research in each jail can be challenging and time consuming. For example, in some situations the sheriff or other top leaders may want to approve all major decisions, while in other situations these leaders may trust those in leadership positions beneath them to handle their duties more independently (see the organizational flowchart for jails in Peak 2016).

While some jails may be approached regularly for research purposes (e.g., perhaps because they are housed in the same area as a university) or may participate in research often because the sheriff values it, in other areas jail staff may not have much experience working with outside researchers. Consequently, the person who takes the researcher's first call may be unsure to whom to refer the researcher (which can also happen in prisons and other organizations). For example, when we initially called jails to request access for our Florida study, we were sometimes transferred and referred to others many times, often from one person to another to another. Often, each successive person to whom we spoke did not know what to tell us or whom to refer us to next. This required us to be patient and persistent in our efforts, which meant starting over with jails' main operator to request a different route (i.e., asking for another person or administrative section of the jail). In such cases, it helped to do some background research on how the jail was organized administratively beforehand. In essence, it is important for researchers to be understanding, yet tireless, in their efforts to get to the right person, as long as research access has not been denied. If access is denied, researchers typically need to attempt gaining access at another jail.

Gaining Access to Parolees and Probationers

There may be multiple ways to access parolees, probationers, and/or the staff that work with them. One way is to access them via the probation or parole agency. However, as with incarcerated populations, this approach requires researchers to be especially careful with IRB protections, since this group also is under correctional control and could potentially face repercussions through the criminal justice system if researchers are not careful.

Depending on the locale, for access to probation officers or clientele, one will first need to determine how the agencies are administered in the location of interest. For example, in some places, probation agencies are administered locally (e.g., California and New York City), and so researchers will need to contact the chief or commissioner of the local probation agency, or at least this office, to start working to obtain access. In other states (e.g., Florida), probation is like parole in that the administration is at the state level, and so access will likely need to be granted at this level before gaining entry into the different offices throughout the state. In these latter cases, there may or may not be an additional step of gaining access in each individual (e.g., regional) office, through the regional or local managers. Parole typically is a state-level function, because it involves people returning from incarceration. Consequently, as with most departments of correction and state-level probation offices, researchers likely will need to obtain access through the state agency first, before going to branch offices. Because official agencies have client databases or lists, taking this approach to access may make sampling easier. For example, one may be able to randomly sample from the population of probation or parole clients. Or, researchers may be able to stratify the sample by location or probation office, if the agency is willing to give the researcher access to the list. If the interest is in studying the officers, a similar approach may be feasible in that one may be able to randomly sample officers or stratify the sample by officer characteristics.

Sometimes, because probationers and parolees are out in the community, researchers may be able to gain access to them without going through the formal criminal justice system. For example, sometimes community-based agencies that serve probation and parole populations will allow researchers access to their clients (e.g., homeless shelters, religious organizations, or nonprofits). In this case, the researcher will need to work with the individual provider to determine the best way to get permission to study the organization's clients. This approach to gaining access may be easier if the formal criminal justice agency is not receptive to outside researchers, but it may preclude the ability to randomly sample and possibly to generalize if the agency granting access only serves a small or particular segment of the probationer or parolee population. That is, there are tradeoffs to each approach to gaining access, and researchers should carefully weigh these issues when deciding how best to go about studying these groups.

Gaining Access to Juvenile Populations

Like adults, juveniles in the justice system may be incarcerated or supervised in the community. Consequently, many of the tips mentioned above regarding how to access adults apply to juveniles—for example, one may need to contact state- or local-level agencies to gain access, depending on the area. However, incarcerated juveniles combine two vulnerable populations for IRB review—prisoners and youth. Specifically, researchers must take even more precautions when studying youths under correctional control. Thus, there may be even more footwork required to gain access to these populations. For example, researchers must generally get both parental consent and youth assent to study youths; meaning that agency permission may not be enough to be able to contact the juvenile clients directly. In some cases, parents may be willing to bring the youth to a research setting and sign consent forms at the time of data collection. In others, researchers will need to meet with the parent to describe the study or send home detailed information and have permission slips completed before contacting the youth. However, for incarcerated youths who are considered wards of the court, there may be "substitutes" for parental permission. For example, a judge may sign an approval, or this can sometimes be done by a participant advocate (someone who is not affiliated with the study or the institution who can assess the ability of the youth; see chapter 4 for information about juvenile parental consent). The key point here is that studying juveniles often requires another layer of gaining access—contacting the agency, obtaining consent from the parent, and then obtaining assent from the juvenile.

Regardless of who researchers work with to gain access, building rapport with the top agency personnel or gatekeepers is critical for building and maintaining positive professional relationships. The following are examples of ways researchers can build rapport with agencies:

- Open (and keep open) the lines of communication.
- Meet with administrators early in the project to discuss the measured outcomes and what constitutes "positive" versus "negative" findings.
- Before finalizing the survey/interview instruments, ask lead administrators responsible for approving the research and possibly other staff if they would like to include any questions (and include them if possible).
- Ask correctional administrators or staff to review the questions for wording and content. They may have suggestions for rewording some questions to get the same information but with less offensive language, should they see some. For example, researchers may be unaware of hidden operational or political issues that could arise if certain buzzwords are used in questions.
- Make as few requests as possible given that your requests usually result in time, work, and paperwork for staff.
- After the conclusion of the project, provide agencies with a report summarizing the findings from your research,

and take into account their comments before sharing the results or report with a wider audience. This agreement may also be included in a memorandum of understanding that is agreed upon during the initial stages of the research (e.g., the approval process). It is often possible to reword statements to convey the same message but in a way that is less offensive to people working in the system. For example, one might say, "guidelines for how to manage clients were unclear" rather than "their leader was a terrible manager who gave no guidance to her staff." Instead of altering *what* is said or infringing upon researcher's freedom of speech, this advice is about considering *how* the message is conveyed to avoid unnecessarily damaging research relationships.

- In publications, acknowledge and thank the agencies and their staff for their participation (unless they prefer not to be identified).

- Send physical or electronic copies of final publications to relevant people in the agency as well as any other relevant leaders and line staff, especially when multiple agencies are involved in the research project or in service delivery. It may be most efficient to have a designated person in the administration who you keep updated on the status of the study and as someone who can help with issues as they arise.

HOW TO ASK FOR PERMISSION TO ACCESS CORRECTIONAL POPULATIONS

Sometimes research requests must be made electronically through an agency's website and other times it will be necessary

BOX 1. EXAMPLE VERBIAGE TO EXPLAIN
REQUEST TO ACCESS JAILS

Hi, my name is [name here]. I am from [name of university here] and I am working on a research project. I am interested in surveying jail inmates about some of their experiences with [insert key focus here]. I would not be asking the inmates anything jail-related. I am hoping to talk with you or someone you recommend I speak with about the possibility of surveying the inmates at your jail.

Adapted from Fox, Lane, and Zambrana (2011)

to call agencies to request access. We highly recommend calling on the phone instead of, or in addition to, e-mailing because e-mails can easily be ignored or unreturned for prolonged periods of time. One useful approach is to send an e-mail first indicating that the researcher will follow up with a phone call in a few days, and then make sure to call within the noted time period. Depending upon the number of facilities from which a researcher will be requesting access, it may be necessary to repeat one's request to conduct research multiple times. For example, given the large number of people with whom we spoke within each jail in our quest to gain access to each location, we found it helpful to have a script prepared (either memorized or read) to briefly introduce ourselves and the purpose of our request. See box 1 for the general verbiage we used when calling jails to request access to conduct research.

Having a typed template or bullet points of what to say helps, because it ensures the caller will not forget anything pertinent.

In addition, if there are multiple people making calls, it ensures that they are at least generally saying the same things. Once connected to the correct person, it is useful to have a longer description of the study (e.g., based on points identified in the informed consent) to help initiate a conversation that can lead to a face-to-face meeting. Sometimes the appropriate contact person may ask researchers to e-mail information first for their perusal before the meeting. In this case, we recommend that researchers summarize their project in a single page for this initial contact because practitioners are often too busy to read the entire proposal. When meeting with gatekeepers, it is important to explain your background, your partnerships with other practitioners, and the products from these partnerships (e.g., bring one-page summaries and copies of technical reports you have prepared). Also in this meeting with gatekeepers, explain your project goals and ask about any goals of the practitioners (Garcia 2016).

TYPICAL STEPS NEEDED TO REQUEST PERMISSION TO ACCESS CORRECTIONAL POPULATIONS

The correctional agency's website or the appropriate person authorized to approve the research should provide instruction on next steps. Many correctional agencies require that researchers submit a number of documents when requesting access, such as:

- A written description of the project on university letterhead and/or a detailed proposal regarding specific information about the research purpose, goals, design, etc.

- Data collection instruments and informed consent forms
- University IRB approval, if this has already been obtained

When one of us was a doctoral student, a jail requested a recommendation letter from our faculty advisor, so there was evidence that someone at the university was supervising the project. Other agencies, like the Texas Department of Criminal Justice, may require a copy of the researcher's driver's license and curriculum vitae (see https://www.tdcj.state.tx.us/faq/faq_external_research.html).

Many correctional agencies require that researchers and research assistants who will enter the facility be given and pass a criminal background check. In our experiences, the background check approval was usually obtained within two to three weeks, although one facility (a jail) took more than three months to get the results and allow us to begin the study. That is, researchers will need to plan for background check waiting periods in their projected study timelines (e.g., for dissertation or grant proposals) and discuss these requirements with agencies of interest up front. Although most facilities we worked with granted approval for the research without requiring a meeting with administrators, we believe it can be very helpful to schedule a meeting prior to data collection (or at least a conference call) to discuss logistics (see chapter 5 for a comprehensive list of questions to discuss with correctional staff prior to data collection). In addition to background checks, some facilities may also require health-related tests, such as tuberculosis testing (e.g., required by the California Department of Corrections and Rehabilitation) or flu shots (e.g., required in our current work with the Department of State Hospitals).

WHEN TO OBTAIN ACCESS TO CORRECTIONAL
POPULATIONS IN CONJUNCTION WITH
OTHER RESEARCH TASKS

Gaining access to correctional populations can take a lot of time, especially if the research participants are minors and under correctional control. If relationships with correctional agencies are not already established prior to the study of interest, we recommend contacting the agencies at the time of idea and instrument creation to discuss the possibility of working with them, as well as discuss any topics the gatekeepers might like you to research for them. In our experience, writing good instruments is not only time consuming but very critical to obtaining methodologically sound results. Researchers may not want to spend time writing and finalizing instruments if the relevant agencies are not interested in participating and the instruments, therefore, may go unused. Yet, agencies are often more invested and willing to help if researchers are also measuring information they need or want.

Original data collection often requires the balancing of a variety of tasks, and the complexity increases when multiple agencies will be accessed. We recommend creating the instrumentation (e.g., survey or interview questions) and informed consent during the same time period that one is calling the facilities to obtain permission to access (steps 1 and 2 in figure 1). If the instrument is nearly complete when seeking agency or facility approval, then items that the practitioners request (if any) can easily be added before applying for university IRB approval. In many of our research projects, we added data collection items to our instruments that were of particular interest to our practitioner partners, even if the information was not specifically relevant to the main aim of the study. In some cases, we have adapted forms to collect additional data if new programming components were implemented after the study had commenced. For example, in our South Oxnard Challenge Project (SOCP), after the program had been running for a while, one staff member took a particular interest in developing job skills in the program's juvenile clients. Consequently, we updated the contact form with a code for job skills. Although we did not have data on job skills training for all youth in the program, we presumably had it for those who received it once it was implemented. Yet, agency interest will vary. For example, in our Florida jail study, we invited administrators to include survey items, but none took us up on this offer. Of course, even if administrators' questions are added to surveys or interviews, only aggregate results can be provided back to them (not individual data). Yet, it may be possible to supply aggregate data for the administrator's particular agency if the number of participants there is large enough that the data would not identify particular individuals.

In many cases, once correctional agencies verbally agreed to approve the research, we requested a letter of cooperation on agency letterhead so we could include these letters with university IRB and funding applications (steps 3 and 4 in figure 1). It should be noted that sometimes it is necessary to apply for funding before or after step 4 (figure 1). We also offered to send correctional agencies a draft letter for this purpose that could be used or modified to save them time and effort, and we found that the agencies often used our exact template (see appendix A for a sample letter). This helped agency staff know what to say and improved efficiency and speed in getting these letters of cooperation. These letters are useful not only for the IRB, but also for dissertation and grant proposals to show readers that the project is well thought out and actually doable. After receiving

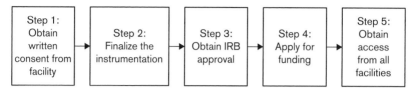

Figure 1. Recommended steps for gaining access to multiple facilities. Source: Fox, Zambrana and Lane (2011)

approval from at least one agency, finalizing the instrument, and obtaining IRB approval, the last step in the access process is securing final approval from any additional agencies that one wants to study (step 5 in figure 1). However, sometimes the IRB will not approve a study without an agency giving a letter of approval, and the agency will not approve the project until it has an IRB approval. In situations like this, we have included in the agency approval letter that the agency approves contingent upon approval by the research organization.

CONVINCING STAFF MEMBERS TO BUY-IN TO THE RESEARCH

Once access to the correctional agency has been granted, the first group to gain buy-in from is staff. Often researchers will need some information from them, whether it is their case files for the participants or information about their own behaviors and attitudes. Often, in big projects like our evaluation of the SOCP, researchers *must* rely on staff to record data for them (typically, to complete extra forms beyond those required by the agency). There must be staff buy-in to ensure this happens. Practitioners and researchers often see research from very different perspectives, and good relationships ensure that researchers and practitioners are better able to work together toward a common goal. In fact, while conducting the SOCP evaluation, we witnessed another funded program in the state come to an almost complete impasse with their research team. At a conference, during a joint panel presentation, the tension and anger between them was palpable, and they were barely willing to speak to each other. The staff from the state agency that provided funds had to be much more hands on to help them work together to complete their longer-term research agreement. This increased the workload for people at the funding agency who were supposed to be monitoring multiple sites. Moreover, the difficulties clearly made the experience less enjoyable for all involved, pointing to the importance of preventing such problems if possible.

Given that building rapport with front-line staff members is key for them to buy-in to the research, we begin this section with specific tips that have worked for us to build and maintain rapport with correctional staff:

- Maintain open communication and ongoing discussions throughout the project, which allows researchers and staff to continually work out issues as they arise. In our projects, we regularly made efforts to ensure the relationship succeeded. As with many multiyear projects, things often changed and open and regular communication made adaptation easier. It also helped to have regular conversations at other times, when there were no issues (have dinner together, ride to meetings together, etc.), because we had broader perspectives on each other than just the daily activities of working on a research project. One of the authors had standing weekly meeting to discuss research-related issues on projects.

- Give practitioners specific information and guidance regarding what you would like from them each time you give a request. For example, it is better to say something like "Please review the survey questions to make sure the wording is appropriate and that we have included all relevant topics" instead of something like "Let me know what you think of the survey."

- Be careful not to undermine staff by making comments or giving the perception that you are aligned too much with offenders (in an effort to gain rapport with participants). That is, try to remain and appear as neutral as possible during the research project. Make sure staff and administrators know you are there to learn from them, not judge them or take sides.

- Make clear that you will be honest in your findings, but that you are not involved in the project to get a specific result, and keep this promise. For example, if you find offenders have negative perceptions of how they are treated inside, assure them that you will report the findings fairly, maybe including perceptions of both offenders and staff. Of course, if you witness actual abuse, your IRB will determine whether researchers are mandated to report it, but this approach is very different from going into a setting with an agenda to find abuse.

- The practitioners and research team should have mutual respect for each other, for their roles, and for differing priorities and pressures, allowing for compromise and discussion about issues rather than both sides relentlessly standing their ground when opinions differ.

- Give line staff who are relied upon for continual submission of data positive reinforcement for completing research tasks (e.g., we used small tokens of appreciation such as a weekly sticker chart and candy or bags of chips for those who turned in all forms on time each month) rather than punishment for not doing it. We did not express frustration to staff when they failed to turn in forms, only continual reminders. We found that peer pressure—seeing who got stickers and candy—actually helped improve weekly submission of data forms (Lane, Turner, and Flores 2004).[1]

Regardless of whether staff are participants in the research, one of the most important lessons is that researchers should focus on the similarities between themselves and the staff rather than differences (e.g., especially not educational, expertise, and attitude differences, unless absolutely necessary to gain access). This helps increase comfort levels. Despite our own advanced degrees, staff members have a lot to teach us about what happens in the everyday world of the justice system. Researchers do not want to alienate staff. These staff often can grant researchers access to a wealth of data that would be off-limits without their connections. In addition, they may be more willing to collect additional data if they feel like they and the researchers are working together as a team on a project rather than having research forced on them. Of course, in some projects, researchers can collect all the data themselves. Yet, in others, without staff cooperation, much data will

---

1. When particular staff refused to submit data forms on time on a regular basis, we did discuss it with management. It was especially useful to remind the management that our reports were better when we had complete data. However, we primarily used positive reinforcement with staff on a daily basis.

BOX 2. BUILDING RAPPORT WITH STAFF WHEN THE RESEARCHER HAS CORRECTIONAL EXPERIENCE

Some researchers who have previously worked in correctional facilities may wonder if and how to leverage this experience when building rapport with correctional staff. For insight on this topic we reached out to one of our colleagues, Carrie Cook, PhD, who is currently an associate professor at Georgia College and State University but worked in a state prison as a counselor prior to obtaining her PhD. Although it was very helpful for Dr. Cook to let administrators and officers know that she had prior correctional experience, she also cautions that this does not automatically give researchers legitimacy with staff. For example, after learning of her correctional experience, one correctional officer replied that Dr. Cook worked in a different facility and that it was "totally different," meaning that Dr. Cook was an outsider at the facility in which she was conducting research. Dr. Cook, who had prior experience as correctional treatment staff, also noticed the "us versus them" mentality between correctional officers—people who "run a dorm in the trenches"—and treatment staff—those who are perceived by correctional officers as having it "easy" (personal communication, Carrie Cook, August 31, 2016). Certainly, establishing legitimacy can be difficult even for someone who has worked in facilities.

Dr. Cook recommends also trying to obtain legitimacy for the research project from a professional association (e.g., American Jail Association, National Sheriff's Association, or another organization). According to Dr. Cook, a "blessing" from a trusted related organization is difficult to get but can be very helpful for gaining access and legitimacy to correctional agencies.

not exist if staff does not cooperate. Researchers cannot be with every staff member every day and must often rely upon these key people to be honest about their activities and to write them down. Correctional staff are also critically important because they are often the gatekeepers to their client caseload. This is particularly critical in studies of juvenile correctional populations because juveniles are impressionable, given that they may be more likely than adults to look to the person managing their case for guidance on what to do. For example, in our SOCP study, we had the case manager (probation officer, mental health counselor, etc.) tell the youths that we would be contacting them to set up an interview. Case managers were supposed to just tell clients to expect to hear from our research team and the managers were not involved in recruitment specifically. However, they sometimes added their thoughts. Some of these case managers were very positive with the youths, indicating that it was no big deal or would be fun, for example. However, one probation officer regularly told his clients that we would be contacting them but then followed it with some version of "But you don't have to do it" or "Don't worry about it." This happened before we were able to remind the youths of the reasons for the study and tell them ourselves about the voluntary nature of their participation (i.e., give them our own informed consent). In this particular situation, we asked the supervisor to ask the officer to approach it differently, but we were unable to change the situation. Consequently, we were able to complete very few interviews with youths on his particular caseload, which meant we had a lot of missing interview data from this group. The bottom line, though, is that this probation officer saw our study as a hassle (because his clients were in the control group and not receiving services) and did not buy-in to the value of the research. He remained hard to convince, although we did work to gain buy-in from the other probation officers in charge of the control group in general.

One way to increase staff buy-in is to listen to and address their concerns. This can be challenging because researchers often do the negotiating with higher-level administrators or heads of agencies, but must work directly with the line staff. Avoiding power struggles even within agencies can be delicate. As one example of how we worked with line staff in the SOCP study, we listened to staff express concern that they would have to complete additional forms that we created for data collection (e.g., contact forms indicating how often they contacted the youths as well as why and where) when they were already overwhelmed with work. While we continued to have the staff for the SOCP complete these forms to document staff contact with youth (see appendices B and C), we created an actual stamp with wooden handle and stamp pad for the control probation officers that allowed them to enter the data in their chronological notes in the youths' files, and the research team then coded the information into contact sheets for data entry (see figure 2). The managers of their units also agreed to allow this information to serve as their records for the typical files, unless other relevant information needed to be added to it. That is, we made it as easy as we could to get the data from staff without imposing too much on their time or daily activities.

Gaining buy-in from peripheral agencies or staff (e.g., people who manage clients in the control group or who provide only a few services, such as contracted educational or drug services) may be tough in many projects. We recommend having initial meetings with the group to describe the importance of the study in detail and answer questions, but also maintaining regular,

Date of Contact:	Duration (in minutes):

Target(s): (circle one)   Youth   Family   Victim
Type of Contact: (circle one) phone   office   residence   workplace school   institutional
collateral contact other _____
Purpose of Contact:

Agency Personnel and Other Professionals Present (e.g., police, therapists):

Is youth in compliance with terms and conditions? (circle one)   yes   no
If no, indicate nature of violation:

Action taken (if filed, indicate California code):
Additional Comments:

DPO Signature:

Figure 2. Contact stamp for staff with client caseloads in the control (routine probation) group in SOCP. Source: Authors

ongoing conversations with relevant staff to ensure all is still going well, monitor their "compliance," quell any concerns, and so on. If there are not researchers on site, we recommend scheduling regular site visits to ensure research staff can monitor daily activities. It also helps at the outset to (1) agree to measure information that would help them or their own agency and (2) to give them regular feedback on the results. One group that often can understand the research value are agency leaders, because they can be convinced that data results can be useful for selling the program or garnering more resources. Sometimes, especially in paramilitary organizations like many corrections agencies, it is helpful to get buy-in from leaders so they can encourage compliance with the research among their staff. In more than one instance, we had to talk to managers to request they "help" get their staff to collect agreed-upon data, complete forms, follow the study protocol, and so forth.

Researchers conducting program evaluations may also need to convince correctional leaders and staff to use random assignment, which means to randomly assign offenders to experimental or control groups. Using random assignment means that subjects have an equal chance of being assigned to either group. Random assignment can occur by doing something simple, such as flipping a coin, or by using random number generators or a computer program with this capability.

Random assignment is considered the "gold standard" for evaluation research (Boruch 1997; Farrington 2003), but it can be difficult to get agencies or their staff to understand the need or to understand that random assignment is legal and ethical. That is, staff may want to use assessments or staff knowledge of client needs to determine who gets access to special programming. In our experience, for example, SOCP staff often wanted to use their personal knowledge about a youth or experience over time in the field to help determine which youths were assigned to which programming rather than rely on luck of the draw. That is, staff may be personally convinced that particular youths need a new or special program and want to bypass any procedure that would leave that assignment to chance. We have found that two points can be convincing to staff. First, random assignment is the fairest way to put youths into groups, if the program cannot serve all people who need the help it provides. It prevents favoritism and ensures all have an equal chance of being selected. Second, random assignment allows for the strongest results, meaning that agency leaders can put more faith in findings than if it were not in place. They can better sell the results, whatever they are, when asking for more funding, for example. Additionally, in some cases, if we had enough degrees of freedom, we allowed a small number of youths to be sent to the project each year (e.g., fewer than 10 percent) while bypassing the random assignment process. These youths, then, are just not to be analyzed for the study but are served by the program.

In our experiences collaborating with staff, we found that some were easier to work with than others, which we expect is typical of most correctional studies. It was important to get to know the personalities and preferences of both the facility and agency administrators and their staffs, because it helped ease the working relationship as we periodically arrived to conduct research. The key, though, was working within the constraints of the facility or agency while trying to maximize our ability to conduct rigorous research. In other words, we were very willing to compromise on details (e.g., times, dates, places to collect data, and managing other idiosyncrasies) of each facility and its staff as long as it did not jeopardize methodological rigor.

With some staff members and in some situations we could be more open about ourselves (e.g., our religious preferences or personal lives) and with others we felt we needed to be more guarded to encourage a smoother working relationship. In our Florida Faith and Community-Based Delinquency Treatment Initiative project, for example, religious beliefs were part of regular conversation among staff, because faith was such an integral part of the program. This meant we had to be especially attuned to our attitudes and how we expressed them, and we could not show judgment when they expressed religious or even political attitudes with which we disagreed.

In this faith project, we also had to be careful about how we responded to behaviors we personally thought were not appropriate. For example, in one facility, we regularly saw areas in physical disarray, such as unmade beds and clothes strewn around, youth jumping across furniture, and expired food (which together signaled to us a lack of good management), while in others important paperwork was not appropriately stored. In one facility, home addresses were listed on youths' bedroom doors, which we thought might be a safety issue for the residents. This facility was later shut down for many problems. While we jotted issues such as these in our research notes, we did not express judgment or report these sorts of problems to their agency managers because we wanted to maintain the working relationships and understand the facilities as they were, not just as they were supposed to be. We allowed the quality assurance process within the agency more broadly to manage the agency's rule enforcement for these issues. Of course, had we seen something abusive or illegal, we would have reported it to the appropriate authorities. If the research team sees something concerning, they should be encouraged to report it to the lead researcher or principal investigator, who may wish to call the university attorneys to inquire about the appropriate course of action (if any) for the researcher.

CONVINCING THE TARGET POPULATION TO PARTICIPATE

Once researchers have obtained agency permission to collect data and secured buy-in from the staff, the next challenge researchers face is often how to convince people to participate. The following is a list of specific tips that have worked for us to build and maintain rapport with participants:

- Make eye contact, be friendly, and treat participants with respect.
- Be careful to use nonjudgmental language, including body language (e.g., avoid crossing/folding arms across your body or making faces).

- Make it clear that you are there because you want to learn from them, that you know they have things they can teach you.

- Reassure them about the informed consent procedures regarding your research and remind them that findings will be reported in a way that does not identify them personally or get either officers or offenders in trouble, unless they threaten to hurt themselves or others.

- Create a comfortable research environment for participants (e.g., minimize distractions, ensure their privacy). Any research situations in which correctional officers appear to punish or negatively regard participants must be immediately terminated to protect participants. Then, the incident will need to be reported to the IRB as an adverse event.

- When opportunities to make small talk arise, discuss general, apparently neutral topics as an easy way to find common ground. For example, major sports teams or events or popular television shows might be topics of easy conversation. Do not provide participants with personal information (e.g., cell phone number or residence location).

- Use humor when appropriate (e.g., when offenders asked if we were afraid to be surrounded by inmates, we smiled and responded confidently and in a lighthearted tone that we were "terrified").

- Genuinely thank participants for their participation and tell them you appreciate their willingness to share their experiences with you.

Another way to think about convincing people to participate in a study pertains to the issue of increasing response rates. Research shows that response rates vary tremendously when researchers request active participation from offenders or staff. For example, response rates among the authors' sample of jail inmates across the facilities we surveyed ranged from 0 percent to 93 percent participation, with an average of 25 percent across fourteen jails (Fox, Zambrana, and Lane 2011). In another Florida study, our surveys among correctional officers across thirteen jails yielded a response rate of nearly 33 percent (Cook and Lane 2012). Although the target population might be a "captive" audience with seemingly little else to occupy their time, this does not necessarily mean that they will agree to participate. Here we offer suggestions for improving participation among offenders.

In our experience, many people in the target population are often willing to participate if approached in the right way. If there are gatekeepers (such as probation officers or facility staff) introducing the study first, it is useful to give them talking points to cover and to ensure they know how important it is to be positive when describing the study. While likely true of many people, correctional populations often respond well to people who appear genuinely interested in hearing their thoughts and opinions. Consequently, researchers expressing genuine interest in a manner that is open (i.e., not judgmental) and warm is very useful in gaining cooperation. Even though the informed consent will likely indicate that the information they provide is either anonymous or confidential, researchers should reiterate it in their own words at the beginning and end of the data collection session, as well as at any point that a participant expresses concern. That is, it can be useful to tell the target population in simple terms that you will not tell anyone what they said, unless they threaten to hurt themselves or someone else. We often informed participants that we would report information based on how many people said each type of answer, which helped them understand how their data might be used without identifying them.

Depending upon the study purpose, consider conducting the research on already assembled groups (e.g., inmates in educational classes or attending religious services) as long as the sample does not generate biased groups (e.g., people incarcerated long term may be more likely to participate). For example, a study on religious attitudes among inmates generally would not want to pull the sample solely from people attending religious services. Compensating participants when possible can incentivize the target population (e.g., with a small donation to their canteen account or a gift card for community population participants).

We often have found that in facilities, the staff member who escorted us had an impact on whether inmates participated in our research. We recommend requesting to be escorted by a friendly officer who is liked and respected by inmates, when possible. On rare occasions when our escort was irritable or abrasive with inmates, we noticed declines in participation. To avoid appearing offensive to jail staff, researchers may wish to ask the administrative contact (e.g., the person who granted approval) in advance of the data collection if there is an officer/staff member who has particularly positive rapport with inmates—or at least who is perceived as fair—who could escort the research team. In facilities, the location of data collection can also matter a lot. Given the coercion necessarily inherent in correctional facilities, it is important that participants feel safe responding to surveys or interviews. Participants are more likely to want to participate in studies if they really believe they can share their attitudes and experiences with the researcher without worrying about how the correctional personnel will respond.

The time of day one collects data can also impact participation rates. In our experiences, conducting data collection later in the day in facilities, if scheduling permits, is better because few inmates are awake (literally or cognitively) when the lights come on in the early morning. In addition, to encourage participation, it is critically important not to schedule data collection during meal times or visiting hours, which are the times people in facilities often look forward to most. Also, it may be important to ask administrators about the educational and employment schedule of inmates, because it is sometimes difficult to pull people from their assignments in order to participate in research.

If conducting original research with community populations (e.g., probationers or parolees), it is also important to consider time of day and place of data collection, to increase the likelihood that the participant will show up. For example, because work is often an important part of terms and conditions, researchers must be flexible to work around their participants' work hours. Scheduling early morning times for data collection may not be ideal in some cases because some participants may prefer to sleep in. Similarly, the meeting location must be convenient for the participant to increase the likelihood of participation. That is, it may be difficult for them to find transportation across town, and so meeting at locations close to their homes or work may facilitate interactions with them. Researchers may need to be creative in this regard. It may be okay to meet at or near their home or in their neighborhood (e.g., in a park), if the researcher feels safe there. Yet, more public places often work, too, especially if the researcher feels safer. These places might include more private areas of fast food or sit-down restaurants, libraries (where one can often schedule a private room for free), or at the probation or parole agency if privacy is available there. Meetings could occur before or after a monthly check-in with the probation or parole officer, for example.

IMPROVING PARTICIPATION RATES OF CORRECTIONAL STAFF

It can be even more challenging to access correctional officers than inmates because correctional staff are very busy and often work twelve-hour shifts. In addition, correctional managers often worry about giving researchers their staff's time away from watching inmates or about paying overtime wages so that staff can participate in research. Even asking for thirty minutes of a correctional officer's time might be a big inconvenience for facility management, especially if the particular institution is understaffed. This is also an issue when correctional staff escort researchers to study inmates, because it takes time away from their regular duties. When studying correctional officers, one approach is to allow staff to participate outside of work time. For example, Dr. Carrie Cook, who studied jail correctional officers, had success by gaining permission to attend shift briefings for short periods of time (between five and fifteen minutes) to introduce and distribute a survey for correctional officers to complete on their own time and mail back to the researcher in self-addressed, stamped envelopes (Personal communication, Carrie Cook, PhD, August 31, 2016). This yielded a 33 percent response rate. Another option for surveys, especially if the researcher cannot provide a self-addressed, stamped envelope in which to return completed instruments, is to provide a locked drop box at the facility or agency office in which respondents can drop the forms. If this approach is chosen, the researcher should be sure that the only people with access to the actual box and its contents are people on the study team. As an alternative way to increase participation, Dr. Cook recommends writing a grant to pay correctional officers for their time to complete research tasks. If funds are more limited, it might be possible to enter participants into a drawing for a gift card (if permitted by IRB regulations). Some staff may be willing to meet with researchers outside of their work day, if it is convenient. For example, they might be willing to meet at a nearby restaurant or coffee shop. Still, like with offenders, if the survey or interview occurs at their workplace, it is important to ensure privacy and confidentiality with answers. That is, researchers will likely get more participation from staff if the respondents feel comfortable that their responses cannot be overheard by others.

IMPROVING PARTICIPATION RATES OF THE FAMILIES OF JUVENILE CORRECTIONAL CLIENTS

Because youths are typically not emancipated but rather exist within families, researchers often may have an interest in studying the family of juvenile correctional clients. Of course, it may be interesting to speak to families of adult offenders or correctional staff also, depending on the research questions. Yet, families of juvenile offenders are often of particular interest to researchers, since youth are typically still living within the context of their family of origin (at least when outside facility walls).

In our own studies, we found, especially in minority communities, that families often felt left out and unimportant in terms of the justice system response. Because they did not feel heard, they often did not express interest initially in being involved in research. In addition, many families of youths in the justice system are struggling themselves, whether with multiple jobs to manage poverty conditions or their own problems. For example, in one case in the SOCP study, a youth was not going to school because the parent had a drug problem and was not doing simple household chores, like washing the youth's clothes for school. Because of the program's approach to addressing multiple problems, the probation officer actually helped the youth do laundry so school attendance could improve. In situations like these, it may be difficult to get families to participate in research, because they are already overwhelmed with other things (and there may be situations like this for families of adult offenders, too).

Still, because families have a lot of information to provide, it is in the benefit of researchers to work hard to help increase their participation. Specifically, if researchers want to survey or interview family members, it is essential to tell them how important their point of view is. That is, researchers can help families feel heard. We often told families that we really wanted to understand the impact of the program on their children, and so we were very interested in their own perceptions of their children as well as their life, delinquency, and justice system experiences. We also offered to meet families wherever and whenever it was convenient (as long as we felt safe in the location). With our open and flexible approach, we often were able to involve people who normally might not want to participate. In the SOCP study, we also had grant funding and were able to reimburse people a little bit (about $15) for their travel and time, which also helped increase participation. Sometimes, in low-income situations, just managing transportation costs can be difficult—even busses may cost too much—and so we attempted to alleviate these concerns to improve participation.

CONCLUSION

Permission to access correctional agencies is an ongoing process, because access can be denied at any time if relationships sour. Relationships with practitioners take a lot of effort, trust, understanding, and willingness to compromise. It is important to remember that building trust is critical, because both correctional practitioners and offenders may have reasons to worry about being open with researchers. And once projects are up and running, it is not uncommon for practitioners and researchers to have very different views of research. In the SOCP study, our views primarily differed in terms of program implementation, data collection, measurement, and reporting procedures and timelines (see Lane, Turner, and Flores 2004 for detailed examples of our differences and how we resolved them). Researchers can work to create ongoing relationships with the practitioner agencies of interest early on and start building the trust, communication, and compromise that we discuss above. As one of our late dear colleagues used to say, "Don't do 'hit and run' research." For example, we maintained positive relationships with agencies by providing aggregate (not the identified) data on topics that interested the agencies.

One general guideline, no matter who is the subject of the research, is to create common ground to put our collaborators and participants at ease to remove barriers to truthful answers.

For example, we introduce ourselves to practitioners and correctional clients by our first names (rather than Professor or Dr.) to facilitate rapport and avoid stuffy titles. However, we are careful to call administrators by their titles (e.g., Captain, Lieutenant) unless instructed otherwise. The ultimate goal is to increase comfort with researchers and other study personnel, so that both cooperation and veracity increase.

The next chapter focuses on the many types of correctional data that can be collected by researchers. This includes utilizing existing data sources, examining agency data, collecting original data, and even using a combination of agency and original data collection methods (e.g., "hybrid" data collection). We also highlight the challenges of measuring recidivism, which is often the outcome of interest by researchers and practitioners. Additionally, the next chapter discusses the helpful skills for different types of data collecting.

CHAPTER THREE

Types of Correctional Data That Can Be Collected

EXISTING MAJOR NATIONAL DATA SOURCES

Many sources of data exist for crime and justice information. Information on arrests and crimes is routinely gathered by the Federal Bureau of Investigation's Uniform Crime Reporting program (https://ucr.fbi.gov/). These data are available to researchers via the Internet and are routinely used to report on changes in crime and arrest trends at the state and national level. The Bureau of Justice Statistics (BJS) operates under the U.S. Department of Justice and collects information on reported and unreported crime from the victim's perspective through the National Crime Victimization Survey (http://www.bjs.gov/index.cfm?ty=dcdetail&iid=245). The BJS also maintains a wealth of information on courts and corrections, with many datasets available online through their website or through the National Archive of Criminal Justice Data, within the Inter-university Consortium for Political and Social Research (ICPSR) (https://www.icpsr.umich.edu/icpsrweb/). A few of the major BJS data collection efforts include the National Prisoner Statistics (NPS) program, Survey of Inmates in Federal Corrections Facilities (SIFCF), and the Survey of Inmates in State Correctional Facilities (SISCF). The NPS has collected data nationally since 1926 on the numbers of prisoners in state and federal prison facilities. The SIFCF and SISCF are surveys of inmates, collected roughly every five years. These contain a great deal of information at the individual level on offender background, current offenses and sentences, and their prior criminal history and services in prison, including treatment and education participation. Because the data are collected at periodic intervals, one can gauge changes over time in a number of variables. The most recent administration of SISCF in 2016 has added a number of health questions, although that data set is not yet available.[1] These surveys represent a national sample of inmates. Of course other study data gathered by individual data collection efforts are also online at ICPSR, and researchers can review the ICPSR website for a myriad of catalogued data sets. The breadth and variety of available data sets preclude our creating a comprehensive table of potential sources, although we feature selected data sources in appendix D. We also recommend that individuals dive into the BJS or ICPSR websites to see what data may be relevant to their research topics. Examining available data sets can also provide background information as a starting point for developing a researcher's own scholarly agenda by suggesting new areas to study or gathering available information in an area of new policy interest.

---

1. The 2004 survey is the latest data available.

USING EXISTING CORRECTIONAL ADMINISTRATIVE DATA

In our studies, we often examine the extent to which we may be able to use data that justice systems are already collecting to help answer research questions. Correctional agencies may track a number of aggregate and individual-level offender data that can be useful for researchers. Recidivism information is often highly desirable as an outcome measure for program evaluations and offender behavior. In many states, official record recidivism data are available via state repositories and federal-level data are available from the Federal Bureau of Investigation. For example, in California, the California Department of Justice maintains automated criminal history records for individuals, and in Florida, the Florida Department of Law Enforcement does the same (see e.g., http://www.fdle.state.fl.us/). Law enforcement, probation, district attorney offices, and courts submit information on arrests and their dispositions. Although mostly used by justice system actors, the information is available to the public for a fee (in Florida) and to researchers through an application process.

These sources of existing data are automated and quite complicated to process (and not always complete), but they can be used to measure arrests, convictions, and sentencing information at the individual level. Corrections agencies themselves collect varying levels of information on their clients in terms of background, risk and need items, program participation, and violations during supervision (in the case of probation and parole). Agencies vary greatly in terms of the quantity and quality of the information collected. Some of these data need to be requested directly from the department. And in some states with automated offender search databases online, a lot of information can be obtained from their public websites if the researchers know the names of people in their samples (e.g., http://www.dc.state.fl.us/InmateInfo/Inmate InfoMenu.asp). In 1998 the Bureau of Justice Statistics sponsored a one-time survey that inventoried state and federal offender-based corrections information systems. That effort showed that most departments of corrections collect a common core of data elements, but not all agencies collect and define elements equally (Association of State Correctional Administrators 1998).

Note that these data are generally collected for management purposes—not necessarily for research purposes. What this can mean is that the data do not contain the depth or type of information a researcher may want, or it may be coded differently than the researcher would prefer. At times the information is available only for the current status of a person (e.g., whether they are currently an inmate or on parole and what their current charge is). In other words, some data are continually overwritten with most recent tracking information for the client, which makes it difficult to trace historical processes that have occurred (e.g., prior statuses, violations, or locations). We have also found that information on referrals to treatment or programming, as opposed to actual service provision, is often more complete, making it difficult to know exactly what treatment offenders actually receive. Even with these restrictions, administrative data may provide a more efficient way to collect information than original data collection. Administrative data may also be helpful to researchers who want to place their own data collection in the context of the larger population they are studying, or to construct a potential comparison group from historical or contemporary offenders.

In our South Oxnard Challenge Project (SOCP) study we studied juveniles on probation and arranged to get "data dumps" regularly from the local agency's data system. Although these data are not always formatted or collected in a way that is conducive to ease of use by researchers, they often provide a wealth of data (e.g., demographic information, prior record, sanctioning and institutional history) that can be modified in format for research purposes. This requires a solid understanding, however, of how the data in their system are coded initially, including any typical errors in data entry that occur. In fact, it is often very useful and important for researchers to go into the actual hard copy of data files of a sample of correctional clients, to ensure that the data in the electronic systems are correct. It is common knowledge that staff often would prefer to work with clients than do paperwork, and so paperwork and data entry may not be as carefully attended to as researchers would prefer. Truly understanding the nature of any data used is critical, because in criminal justice studies the results may be used to make policy. In other words, results may affect real lives, and so reporting accurate results is absolutely crucial. Understanding and managing major data sets from agencies is an important skill for people interested in doing many types of correctional studies. If the primary researchers do not have these skills, they should consider partnering with scholars who do when access to these data sets is required.

As another example, we have also worked directly with the Florida Department of Juvenile Justice (DJJ) to obtain juvenile records, working with their research team. Because the youths' official records were housed in a central database at the state level at the DJJ, we were able to work directly with analysts to garner downloads of youths' records across all institutions, meaning generally we did not need to bother each facility for their youths' files on a consistent basis. Regular downloads from the state database were more efficient and allowed for more consistent data across participants compared to obtaining the data from each facility. We gave the DJJ research staff with access to the central database the names, birthdates, and facilities where youths were housed, so that we could obtain a dedicated research file with their official records in them. We then stripped the files of the names, and entered a study code for each youth to ensure the youths' privacy. With automated data there is some small time period where the files actually have the ID. This necessitates that a link list be stored either encrypted on the computer server or deleted from the server/computer.

PROS AND CONS OF COLLECTING YOUR OWN DATA

Although there are certainly data sets that one can obtain through ICPSR, or other repositories, many students and researchers prefer to gather data themselves from individuals in the system. Quite a variety of subject populations are available to address research questions. These include inmates and probation and parole clients as well as juveniles managed by the system, and line staff, such as correctional officers, parole agents, and probation officers. Teachers and other prison program staff, management staff at prisons (e.g., wardens), and staff at state headquarter agencies (secretaries of departments of corrections) each provide distinctive viewpoints that are important to examine in their own right.

Interviews

As we have noted, interviews and surveys are popular methods of collection for original data and have been for decades. For example, Newman (1958) described the importance of interviewing in prison, conditions for success, and rapport building, which are many of the topics we also discuss. Interviews provide perhaps the richest form of in-depth data, as interviewers can delve deeper into details of questions asked and make sure that questions are understood appropriately by offering clarification when needed. Interviews are especially valuable if the researcher is able to tape record the session; however, one must be careful that the use of a tape recording does not increase distrust (Roberts and Indermaur 2008). Not only do interviews, once transcribed, provide a check on interviewer notes, but they also provide direct quotes, which can be used to provide rich context when discussing results. However, interviews are time intensive. As a result, sometimes samples are smaller than would be gained from a survey, and a smaller sample in some cases can lead to trouble generalizing to the population. In addition, interviews require private interviewing areas, which can involve movement of inmates or meeting people in the community in public at quiet areas or at probation, parole, or juvenile justice system offices.

Surveys

Surveys can often be administered to collect similar information as interviews and can potentially be collected on larger numbers of participants given a fixed amount of time the researcher is able to be on location (e.g., at a prison, jail, juvenile detention center, parole/probation office). However, surveys also have limitations in that they are often group administered, and individual attention for understanding may be less than in one-to-one interviews. Surveys may be better in situations in which the researcher feels a larger sample size might be more important than depth of understanding. There is no "right" or "wrong" method for researching correctional populations. Rather, there are a series of trade-offs the researcher must make. See Dillman, Smyth, and Christian (2014) for user-friendly and practical advice for designing surveys.

Although research may be done at only one particular point in time, many research questions or projects are longitudinal in nature. This requires that the researcher return to the same individuals to re-interview or re-survey at a later point in time. Nothing is worse than making the mistake of not obtaining enough information to locate an individual for subsequent contact.[2] Follow-up is an extremely time-consuming and expensive component of research, especially for individual-level interviews. Although it is difficult to calculate the cost per interview, we often refer to longitudinal interviews as the "Cadillac" research design—meaning it is the most costly.

Focus Groups

In the beginning stages of research, we find that the use of focus groups and observation may be particularly advantageous. Focus groups consist of small groups of people, usually between eight and ten participants, with a facilitator leading the discussion of specific topics (Krueger and Casey 2014). We are also currently involved in evaluating Arts in Corrections (AIC) programs. Because relatively little strong empirical work has been done on these programs (in fact, people will often laugh when we say we

---

2. We briefly discuss tracking participants over time in chapter 4's section on protecting participants' identities.

are evaluating AIC), we began with focus groups of inmates both in prison and recently released individuals in the community, asking a series of questions that were designed to help us understand the "change mechanism" of AIC that may help offenders return successfully to the community. Our focus groups ask a number of questions derived from criminological theories (e.g., social learning) to understand what may be occurring as offenders prepare for and act in dramatic work, learn skills to create visual art, or participate in music performances.

Observations

Finally, observation of behaviors of inmates and correctional staff may provide insights and background for further study. Observational studies have advantages in that they may not require informed consent (if no intervention with participants is taking place), and are perhaps the easiest logistically to arrange. For example, we observed Thinking for a Change (T4C) groups in juvenile institutions, as part of a process evaluation (for a description, see the National Institute of Corrections website, http://nicic.gov/t4c). Because the structure of the lessons was to be the same each time, despite different content, we created an observation coding form that allowed us to collect data on each observed lesson (see the T4C facilitator peer rating form in appendix E). We created a very similar form to allow the facilitators of the T4C group to rate themselves as well as the co-facilitators. Still, in many cases if there is no coding form or if additional notes are taken, the real "work" of observational studies can take place after data collection as the researcher works with the data coding to uncover themes and theory that best explain the observations.

PROGRAM EVALUATION

Arguably one of the most important types of studies conducted by people who do research with correctional populations is program evaluation, which may incorporate any or all of the types of original data collection or secondary data analysis we have discussed. There are a number of how-to books to explain how to do this type of study (Rossi, Lipsey, and Freeman 2004). We recommend working in collaboration with experienced evaluators if one is less experienced in doing this type of study, because they are often major undertakings.

The general goal of program evaluation is to determine whether a program or approach to managing or treating correctional populations is effective. Policymakers, practitioners, stakeholders, academics, and many others are often interested in knowing whether a program is helping (or hurting) its clients, and if a program needs revision or improvement. Policymakers are often especially interested in knowing how effective programs are because they must make decisions about how to distribute a limited amount of money when faced with multiple requests for funding. That is, practitioners and policymakers in recent years have focused on what is now called evidence-based programming (or criminal justice approaches that have data and results to support their use) and many requests for proposals (RFPs) for funding require program evaluation as a part of program funding (see MacKenzie 2000; Office of Justice Programs 2016).

Because the ultimate goal of program evaluation is to determine effectiveness, we believe these research projects *must* incorporate collaboration and partnership with agency leaders and staff (e.g., to allow access to sites, clients, and databases and collect data) from the conception of the study, typically also need cooperation from clients (or offenders) to participate in data collection efforts, and require intensive effort on the part of researchers. Rarely can researchers in these studies simply request data, clean it, and analyze it. Rather, we argue that the best evaluations in correctional research involve at least both process evaluation and outcome evaluation and much hands-on effort from researchers over time.

Outcome evaluations typically focus on how the program affects clients, using such measures as recidivism (self-report and officially documented), drug use and abuse, employment, education, and life skills. Process evaluations answer questions related to what the program is actually doing, which is critical to explaining any outcome results. That is, process evaluations measure implementation of the program, including measuring whether the program is reaching its intended target population and delivering the program as it was designed to be delivered (see Rossi, Lipsey, and Freeman 2004). To understand how well a program is being delivered, it is best (but expensive) to immerse project researchers in the study context (i.e., to spend as much time as possible on site observing, talking to people, taking notes, and collecting data). This approach helps the research truly understand the context of the project, the successes and hurdles faced in implementation, the attitudes and efforts of staff, and the experience of people who work in and are treated by the program, and ensure that data collection is being done appropriately and efficiently. This information is critical to understanding what results mean in terms of outcomes for clients. For example, if a program is not being implemented well, it is hard to say that evidence of no impact on clients means the program itself does not work. Rather, it may be that the program was never implemented as planned due to issues such as lack of training, staff turnover, or other hurdles faced by the program. Without knowledge of how the program actually worked, it is hard to know why programs do or do not work when outcomes are assessed.

Evaluation projects can also include efforts to assess the need for a proposed or current program, assess program theory, and measure program efficiency (see Rossi, Lipsey, and Freeman 2004). Sometimes correctional researchers also conduct these studies, but they are not as often the key focus of published studies. In some cases, for example, researchers work with agency leaders and program staff prior to submitting joint grant proposals to help collect information on the need for specific types of programming in correctional institutions or communities and help them develop the program model (theory) to guide program development and implementation. Other times researchers are brought into the program after these have been developed and the program has been funded, and therefore must assess the results of the program model and design that has already been established without their input. This can be harder, because the program model may be more abstract or less appropriate to the target population than would be ideal. For example, agency leaders and practitioners sometimes hear of interesting or "hot" ideas (e.g., from their trade magazines or other agency leaders) but do not have the academic knowledge base to necessarily know of specific nuts and bolts to include in their proposals to make their concepts easier to measure. As we have noted in other sections of this book, the earlier collaborations are forged, the easier studies tend to be over time.

Efficiency analysis focuses on cost-benefit or cost-effectiveness and may be less common in correctional research because cost data are not available in the form necessary to do this type of analyses, because some researchers may not have the type of economic expertise to do cost-benefit analysis, and because we are often taxed by efforts to collect and analyze all the data necessary to do the process and outcome evaluations (see Roman 2013; Rossi, Lipsey, and Freeman 2004). Yet, cost-benefit (where outcomes are reported in monetary terms, such as dollars saved by preventing victimization) or cost-effectiveness analysis (where outcomes are reported without dollar amounts, such as how much it costs to keep someone in prison for a year and therefore incapacitate offenders) can be very useful to policymakers and other stakeholders who must make budgetary decisions (see Rossi, Lipsey, and Freeman 2004). In some large grant-funded studies, it may be possible to hire an economic consultant to do these analyses if they are desirable and the lead researchers do not have the expertise to do it themselves.

The Washington State Institute for Public Policy (WSIPP) is one of the nation's leading organizations doing cost-benefit analyses of correctional programs. Their approach includes meta-analyses of the literature to determine whether programs work; a cost analysis to determine whether benefits outweigh costs, followed by a sensitivity analysis of findings. If researchers are unable to perform their own cost analyses, findings from WSIPP various program reviews can provide some useful information.

COLLABORATING WITH AGENCIES FOR HYBRID DATA COLLECTION

One of the most creative options we have used to collaborate with agencies is what we refer to as "hybrid" data collection, which is especially useful in many program evaluation efforts. In our SOCP study, we worked with the probation agency to develop new forms for probation officers to complete. This served our research purposes as well as the agency's management needs. The form was completed by probation officers and the data were sent to us. Thus, we were able to leverage the efforts of both the probation agency and the research team.

As another example, in an evaluation of a pilot parole decision-making tool for violations in California, we worked on a group effort with the Division of Adult Parole and the Center for Effective Public Policy that created a computer program that would assist the agents in gathering the information required for the decision-making tool, the recommendations of the tool, and the sanction that was selected (see CDCR press release: http://cdcrtoday.blogspot.com/2008/10/california-to-launch-parole-violation.html). This computer program was developed separately from the main operational parole tools and data systems, but ultimately was incorporated in CDCR routine operations. The collaborative effort did require someone in parole with expertise in database programming to assist the effort. For our research purposes, we were provided with data "dumps" for analyses to determine for whom and how well the tool was implemented (see Turner et al. 2012). From a researcher's point of view, this effort was only partially successful. The use of a tool to automate decisions, which had traditionally been based on individual parole agent's clinical judgment, was met with quite a bit of resistance. Although training sessions were held with staff, parole agents felt the tool did not adequately capture the elements they used to make revocation decisions. This resulted in agents either choosing a more serious or less serious sanction than recommended by the tool in 30 percent of the cases. This was unfortunate for testing the fidelity of the pilot program; however, the database was helpful in collecting the data to show this less-than-preferred level of buy-in by agents (Murphy and Turner 2009).

HOW TO MEASURE RECIDIVISM

Recidivism is arguably the most common metric used to measure success of offenders and programs (see Maltz's [1984] seminal work). For being so ubiquitous, it is curious that there is no agreed-upon definition of what recidivism means. One can imagine why this is the case. Different segments of the justice system have different metrics for their own success. For law enforcement, arrests are most relevant. Prosecutors may prefer "filed charges." Probation and parole often consider whether an offender has successfully completed supervision with no supervision violations. Prisons often consider whether the inmate has returned to incarceration. Researchers may want to know not only about "officially" recorded events, such as arrests, convictions, and incarcerations, but also about actual criminal behaviors. For this, self-report is required.

As an example of how difficult defining recidivism can be, we discuss a recent effort by the state of California to determine an official state definition of recidivism. Legislation passed in 2013 required the state, among other things, to develop definitions of key terms, including "recidivism." The effort was led by the California Board of State and Community Corrections (BSCC), which consulted with a number of stakeholders and experts, including a county supervisor or county administrative officer; a county sheriff; a chief probation officer; a district attorney; a public defender; the secretary of the California Department of Corrections and Rehabilitation; a representative from the Administrative Office of the Courts; a representative from a nonpartisan, nonprofit policy institute with experience and involvement in research and data relating to California's criminal justice system; and a representative from a nonprofit agency providing comprehensive reentry services.[3] One of us also served as a representative from the "nonpartisan agency" constituency. The group worked together for eleven months to craft a definition, after a series of meetings, in which different agencies argued strongly (from the author's point of view) for measures that were aligned with their own constituency groups. The group finally voted 8–2 in favor of a single definition based on convictions over a three-year period, but hedged their recommendations with the addition of supplemental measures:

Adult Recidivism Definition

- Recidivism is defined as a conviction of a new felony or misdemeanor committed within three years of release from custody or committed within three years of placement on supervision for a previous criminal conviction.

Supplemental Measures

- This definition does not preclude other measures of offender outcomes. Such measures may include new arrest, return to custody, criminal filing, violation of supervision, and the level of offense (felony or misdemeanor).

Recidivism Rates

- While the definition adopts a three-year standard measurement period, rates may also be measured over other time intervals such as one, two, or five years.[4]

3. http://leginfo.legislature.ca.gov/faces/billCompareClient.xhtml?bill_id=201320140AB1050
4. Board of State and Community Corrections California, "BSCC Committee Releases Recidivism Definition," press release, November 13, 2014,

Ironically, just before the BSCC press release, the California attorney general released an alternative definition of recidivism aimed at law enforcement stakeholders:

- An arrest resulting in a charge filed by a prosecutor within three years of an individual's release from incarceration or placement on supervision for a previous criminal conviction.[5]

In addition to the differences in the definition of the event that defines recidivism, the timeframe in which a recidivism event occurs is also not standard. A common time frame, as illustrated above, is three years. The Bureau of Justice Statistics has collected the recidivism of state prisoners about once a decade since 1983.[6] They used a three-year follow-up for the first two waves of data collection and a five-year follow-up for the 2005 sample. In reality, researchers and scholars must necessarily use recidivism data that are available to them. For example, in evaluating programs, clients and policy makers may want to have results as soon as possible. There are a number of cases in which the authors of this book have used relatively short timeframe—six to twelve months—for recidivism analyses.[7] In the SOCP, we followed youths for more than two years post–random assignment

http://www.bscc.ca.gov/downloads/Recidivism%20Defintion%20Press%20Release.pdf.

5. Office of the Attorney General, State of California Department of Justice, (October 16, 2014). "Attorney General Kamala D. Harris Releases Proposed Statewide Definition of Recidivism," press release, https://oag.ca.gov/news/press-releases/attorney-general-kamala-d-harris-releases-proposed-statewide-definition.

6. Three separate data efforts have been done: 1983, 1994, and 2005)

7. See RAND reports prepared yearly for Los Angeles County Juvenile Justice and Crime Prevention Act programs. The most recent report by Fain, Turner, and Greathouse (2015) is located on the RAND website: http://www.rand.org/pubs/research_reports/RR1023.html

(Lane et al. 2005). Often, determining how to measure recidivism requires balancing many factors, including funding, timeframe for a project, and data availability.

Just as there is no standard definition of recidivism, there is no standard way to analyze recidivism outcomes. Many studies use a binary measure for an outcome of interest (e.g., "any" arrest or conviction) over a standardized time period, say three years. Others use the number of recidivism events, such as the number of arrests. If one is interested in an *arrest rate* for an individual (or group), a researcher can calculate this by using the number of arrests divided by the time an individual is "at risk" for the recidivism event (e.g., the calculation of lambda, or offense rate, was central to groundbreaking work conducted at RAND on identifying the high rate offender; see Chaiken, Chaiken, and Peterson 1982 and Greenwood and Abrahamse 1982). In this case, it is important for the researcher to be able to calculate the "street time" the individual has over the standardized time period. For example, if someone were incarcerated for one year of a three-year period, the researcher would need to subtract that time period from the denominator in calculating a rate. One may also measure the "most serious" event for recidivism, which may be especially relevant when trying to understand the severity of recidivism. "Time to recidivism" or "time to failure" analyses are more nuanced than other measures in that they take into account the timing of the recidivism event (e.g., whether it occurs sooner or later during a follow-up period). More recently, the environment has been considered in recidivism analyses, recognizing the importance of neighborhood in understanding recidivism (see Kubrin and Stewart 2006). The choice of measures can be driven by the availability of data, but more importantly, should be driven by the researcher's hypotheses.

The different approaches also require different statistical techniques. Binary outcomes can be tested using chi-square tests or logistic regression models. Continuous outcomes are often analyzed with Poisson or negative binomial regression models that take into account the often non-normal distribution of the outcomes. Cox proportional hazard models are often used for time-to-failure analyses (Cox 1972); hierarchical linear models are used when individuals are nested within neighborhoods or other larger units (Raudenbush and Bryk 2002).

Related to the measurement of recidivism is agreement on what constitutes a "good outcome." Many of us assume that higher recidivism rates are "worse" than lower rates. However, this is not always the case. In the nationwide experimental evaluation of intensive supervision probation and parole (see Petersilia and Turner 1993), we had a number of awkward conversations with our participating probation departments as we were discussing our findings. Our study results showed that experimental groups had higher recidivism rates than comparison group offenders who received "business as usual" supervision. We interpreted this as a negative finding. However, probation key actors felt this was a "good" outcome, because they were able to "catch" the experimental group more often. We recommend that, when working with an agency, discussions occur early in the collaboration about which measures are of particular interest to the agency and which direction of the outcomes are considered "good" and "bad" results.

Finally, we have also been in the awkward position of using multiple outcome measures, only to have them contradict each other. In the RAND randomized experiment evaluating the Paint Creek Youth Center (PCYC)—a private alternative to juvenile state-level facilities—we utilized both official record and self-report measures for recidivism. In analyzing outcomes, official record information suggested that the program was successful; however, self-report measures of crime suggested the program was less successful. We were at a loss of how to explain the difference in findings, however, program staff suggested a possible explanation. Part of the PCYC program was to work with youth so they would be more truthful; staff suggested that PCYC were simply being more honest than control youth in admitting criminal behavior during the study follow-up (Greenwood and Turner 1993).

DATA ANALYSIS SKILLS NEEDED FOR DIFFERENT TYPES OF DATA GATHERING

As a rule of thumb, we often suggest that the level of effort and time for data analyses is inversely related to the closeness the researcher has to the actual collection of the data. This means that using administrative data sets can be incredibly time consuming for a number of reasons. Administrative data are notoriously messy. In many systems, a number of individuals may be entering data, resulting in reduced interrater consistency. Data are often missing and codebooks are often inadequate or unavailable. Data from multiple sources must often be merged. However, one of the most difficult challenges may be lining up the administrative data in a way that satisfactorily answers the research questions. For example, answering a question about a prison policy's effect on offender safety using official record data may not provide information on actual incidents—just those that are officially reported to authorities. Working with administrative data sets often takes very good programming and sleuthing skills. Preliminary work getting the data ready for the analysis is what takes a great deal of time and is often not very much "fun." We say that 90 percent of the researcher's effort goes into getting the data clean (e.g., creating codebooks, cleaning the data, and ensuring interrater consistency) and 10 percent for statistical analyses.

Data that are collected using the researcher's own interviews or surveys are generally much easier to work with since a tremendous amount of thought and care has gone into the effort *before* data collection. Of course, these kinds of data can bring with them the usual concerns, such as interviewer or coder reliability and missing data. In general, the researcher has more control over these issues in the training of interviewers/staff and gathering of information.

CONCLUSION

This chapter outlines the great variety of data that can be used to address research questions or policy impacts. Types of data range from that already collected by others and often maintained in data archives available to the public to original data collected by the researchers. It is important not to rule out one or the other automatically; each has advantages that may benefit the study. Original data collection can take many forms, including personal interviews, observation, surveys, and administrative data. One thing to remember is that the researcher may be able to leverage his or her efforts by partnering with an agency for data collection, or building upon data collection efforts already developed by an organization for their own purposes. As a word of advice, original data may have few data quality and analysis issues to contend with—administrative data from agencies are often quite complicated, often poorly documented, and often require a great deal of massaging, requiring sophisticated data analytic and programming skills. Finally, not everyone agrees on the definition of one of the major outcomes researchers use to measure offender behavior or program success—recidivism. It is best to make sure all parties are in agreement before the project starts on how this will be measured and what direction indicates success.

With an understanding from the current chapter of the types of data that are available when researching correctional populations, we turn our attention in the next chapter to issues related to the safest and most appropriate ways for collecting those data. Maintaining research ethics and navigating the informed consent process can have special challenges when studying correctional populations. The following chapter highlights important considerations and tips for obtaining institutional review board approval and maintaining safety for everyone involved in the research project (e.g., client participants, correctional staff, and researchers).

CHAPTER FOUR

Informed Consent Process and Research Ethics

IRB APPROVAL FOR DIFFERENT TYPES OF DATA GATHERING

Federal regulation guidelines are provided by 45 CFR 46 and define three levels of institutional review board (IRB) review: exempt, expedited, and full committee review. Individual IRBs follow the federal regulations, but may have institution-specific policies about level of review. Basically, the higher the level of risk to the person studied, the higher the level of review required. Without a doubt, the most sensitive research projects in corrections are those that collect self-reported information (e.g., interview, survey, or focus groups) from incarcerated offenders—whether they are in prisons, jails, or juvenile facilities. Inmates are considered vulnerable populations for human subjects research and require full committee review by IRBs. Researchers must carefully delineate the risks and benefits for participation. One of the qualifications for research approval on prisoners is that participation cannot have any impact on consideration for parole. For this reason, researchers must protect participants' identities, which includes minimizing knowledge of inmate participation and by preventing any influence of study findings on parole boards' decisions. This often requires careful discussion of how participants are recruited, how they are interviewed, and how their information is protected from a breach of confidentiality. Thus, a researcher who wishes to propose an in-prison project must be prepared for a rather extended IRB process.

Using administrative data can involve a simpler IRB process, especially if the data are deidentified (meaning there is no way to identify to whom the data apply). We have found that inmate data (official record files only) can qualify for expedited review in some cases, moving the IRB process along more quickly. We must still, however, carefully delineate handling, processing, storage, and reporting of data.

Understanding one's rights and what exactly is being agreed upon can be confusing for participants. For example, there can be confusion between participants getting an intervention versus signing up for a study. Participants may think they need to consent to data collection to receive a treatment. To help researchers clearly navigate IRB issues related to informed consent, this chapter highlights topics such as safety, coercion, ethics, disclosure, IRB advice, and gaining parental consent/assent to study incarcerated juveniles.

HOW TO AVOID HARM TO OFFENDERS, CORRECTIONAL STAFF, AND RESEARCHERS

Research is guided by three main principles from the Belmont Report: safeguards must be in place to promote (1) *respect* for people, especially those with "diminished autonomy" such as correctional populations, (2) *beneficence,* or an obligation to maximize benefits and minimize harm, and (3) *justice* in terms of distributing benefits and harms of research (see U.S. Department of Health and Human Services 1979). In the United States, human subjects research is guided by federal and state regulations, with IRBs in universities and other private sector organizations responsible for review and approval of research projects. People who are incarcerated are officially considered to be vulnerable populations, which requires researchers to implement additional safeguards for their protection. Although each research organization has different procedures and protocols for approving research with offenders, inmates, and correctional staff, many guidelines and policies are similar across various university and correctional institutions. It may come as a surprise to some readers that IRBs and their processes are set up for the protection of the *research subjects.* They are not set up for the protection of those conducting the research. In this chapter, we review different types of harm that can arise in conducting research with correctional populations, including those inside and outside of institutions. We address issues covered by human subjects considerations as well as harms that may be experienced by the researchers themselves. While plenty of advice exists elsewhere about how to avoid harm in general, there are some unique situations that may arise when studying offenders or correctional officers in particular, which is the focus of this chapter.

It is generally safe to conduct research with correctional populations, especially in institutions where officers are there to provide safety. Even so, researchers will be concerned with preventing harm to offenders, correctional officers, and themselves. Each researcher may have different perspectives and perceptions about their own personal safety while inside the correctional setting and while interacting with offenders. Just as with fear of victimization in general (Lane et al. 2014), researchers' fear and safety concerns while "inside" or while conducting research with probationers and parolees may depend upon a variety of personal and professional experiences. Of course, all safety concerns should be taken seriously.

We first discuss reducing potential harms in correctional institutions. Depending on the correctional institution, there are likely to be a variety of safeguards that can be utilized to reduce or avoid potential risk. While the authors of this book have not personally felt afraid while on the inside, in order to feel safe we each have worked with correctional institutions to employ safety measures (e.g., correctional officer escorts, limiting offenders' access to research materials, maintaining a comfortable distance from offenders when necessary). It is important for researchers entering correctional facilities and interacting with correctional populations to feel comfortable doing so and, if not, the researchers (or their research assistants) should not pursue this type of research.

SAFETY OF THE RESEARCH TEAM INSIDE CORRECTIONAL FACILITIES

Some correctional facilities have a strict "no hostage policy," which means that the correctional facility will not bargain with inmates under any circumstances, even if inmates have taken a hostage. To be clear, no hostage policies mean that hostages may be harmed or even killed by anyone (e.g., by inmates or by others if the institution decides to use force to attempt to rescue the person from inmates). Prior to data collection, researchers entering correctional facilities may wish to obtain information regarding any hostage policies of the facility. This information should also be clearly communicated to any research assistants so they can decide whether they are comfortable with the research duties and potential risk. However, in our experience, staff in institutions take extra care to protect outsiders inside the walls. Hostage taking is a rare occurrence, but it is a possibility.

Collecting data within correctional facilities means that researchers often walk among large groups of inmates. For example, in every facility we entered in our jail study, we were almost constantly in close enough proximity such that numerous inmates could have simply reached out to touch us at any time. This was also true in studies we have done in juvenile facilities. This was different from some of our experiences conducting research in prison, where we were typically—but not always—more removed from inmates (e.g., behind glass walls or across the table from inmates who were handcuffed in some way). The close distance to inmates may result in the following special considerations for researchers.

Balancing Participant Benefits with Researcher Safety

Depending upon the correctional facility, researchers may be able to request that staff remain inside or outside of the room during data collection. Asking correctional staff to remain outside of the room may increase participants' perceptions of privacy and comfort level, which may lead to higher participation rates, reduced feelings of coercion, and more valid responses to research questions. However, some researchers may not feel as comfortable or as safe without a correctional officer nearby. If researchers will be locked in dorms with inmates and no staff member (which we frequently requested), we highly recommend communicating with correctional officers early and often about their whereabouts during data collection (e.g., immediately behind the door versus down the hallway out of earshot). Researchers can often use personal safety devices provided by the institution to call for assistance, if needed.

There may also be a middle ground between officers located outside of the room versus too close for the comfort of participants. Some jails and prisons have surveillance areas in which correctional officers observe inmates from behind a glass wall, and most have video surveillance of all areas. Others have dorms so large that correctional staff can remain a fairly far distance from the research. These alternatives may provide ideal situations for researchers who wish to be monitored by staff but from a distance. In our experience conducting research in jails, some required a staff member to remain in the room with us, while others allowed us to collect data without staff present. In one jail that accommodated our request for the correctional officer to remain outside of the room, we were given a "man down beeper," and we were to press a button if we perceived danger. Although researchers need to be safe and aware at all times, we have yet to feel afraid while in jails or prisons.

What to Do If an Inmate Touches You

In our encounters with more than an estimated 10,000 jail and prison inmates, we have never been the recipients of unwanted touching by inmates. We believe it to be highly unlikely, yet possible, for researchers to be touched by an inmate in an inappropriate manner. In the case of accidental or minor touching (e.g., brushing hands when handing out or back pencils or surveys), we recommend discreetly creating distance from the inmate and displaying minimal reaction. Depending upon the situation and any threat or danger that researchers perceive, it may be appropriate to (a) do nothing and continue with data collection by ignoring the behavior, (b) politely request the behavior stop, (c) terminate the inmate's participation, or (d) terminate the data collection session. In our experience, correctional officers may also be attuned to inmate behaviors when visitors (such as researchers) are in the facility, and so officers may take care of the situation themselves (e.g., warn the inmate, ask the inmate to go this/her room, or remove the inmate from the situation entirely). Although officers may solve the problem before the researcher needs to, we highly recommend thinking through this issue in advance and remaining calm if the situation ever presents itself. Box 3 features different ways researchers might decide to handle being touched by an inmate, along with example verbiage for navigating these potentially uncomfortable situations.

What to Do If You Are Accidentally Locked Inside a Dorm Alone with Inmates

While we recommend using the buddy system when collecting data in jails and prisons (meaning having more than one person at each data collection session), unexpected situations may occasionally arise that separate researchers from each other and from correctional staff. On one occasion inside a Florida jail, we were separated from our research assistant when one correctional officer began escorting us into a dorm while another correctional officer called to us from behind to talk. This resulted in one of us being detained by correctional staff outside of the

BOX 3. EXAMPLES OF HOW TO RESPOND TO AN INMATE TOUCH

Researcher's course of action when touched by an inmate	Example verbiage
How to politely request the behavior stop	"I would appreciate it if you please did not touch me."
How to respond if an inmate apologizes	"Thank you."
How to respond if an inmate asks why you have asked them not to touch you	"Touching makes me feel uncomfortable and it is against the facility's rules. Are you ready to continue participating in the research?"
How to terminate the inmate's participation	"I am sorry that we need to have you stop participating in this study because you touched me. May I please have your survey materials?"
How to terminate the data collection session for a group of participants	"I am sorry that we need to stop this study now. We will continue after a short break / We will not be continuing. May I please have your survey materials?"

dorm while our research assistant was locked inside the dorm alone with dozens of inmates and without the presence of a correctional officer. In situations like these—as with most uncomfortable situations—the best course of action is to *remain calm*. While we calmly yet seriously (not in a jovial way) requested that correctional staff quickly escort our research assistant out of the locked dorm, our research assistant calmly waited by the door while she was approached and greeted by inmates. The inmates also were surprised to see her (an unannounced visitor without any correctional escort) and they began asking who she was and what she was doing there. She calmly introduced herself and explained that another researcher would soon enter to introduce a research project. Remaining calm and collected in uncomfortable situations may help defuse any danger with the added benefit of demonstrating that the researchers are unafraid of inmates, which helps establish rapport. On the inside, to show fear is to show weakness (Toch 1975) and we made concerted efforts to exhibit relaxed confidence. In addition, in some cases, officers are likely watching via video surveillance, and so the researcher may not be physically "alone." Researchers may wish to inquire about camera surveillance inside the facility before collecting data.

SAFETY WHEN RESEARCHING COMMUNITY SAMPLES

Conducting research with offenders in the community presents its own set of safety challenges, especially for researchers. Researchers may be afraid to go into certain communities due to high crime or environmental cues, such as disorder or diversity, which may make it feel like an unsafe area (see Lane et al. 2014).

Or, they may be afraid to meet people who have been convicted of committing crime. Personal safety is of the utmost importance, and researchers must use their own experience, knowledge, and "gut" feelings to guide their forays into particular neighborhoods, buildings, and so on.

Yet, there are some general guidelines that can help increase safety. For example, researchers should have dedicated phones (e.g., "burners") and e-mails used for contact with research participants, so that their personal information (phone number, address, e-mail address, etc.) is not available to the participant. In fact, whether doing research inside or outside institutions, researchers should be careful not to share much personal information with participants. However, they should also not appear closed off or unapproachable by refusing to tell offenders anything at all. It might be okay to say that one has children but not share information such as the child's name or school. Or, it might be okay to name the university associated with the research (which is usually part of IRB consent forms) or what one's career goals are (e.g., to become a professor) or why one is studying people in corrections (e.g., research interests) but not to say when classes are held, in what buildings, or where one studies at what times. Of course, these examples are general suggestions. Researchers must use their own judgment and err on the side of caution, keeping safety in mind at all times (see "Disclosing to Participants Other Information Related to the Research" below for strategies on tactfully declining to answer personal questions).

In addition, meetings with offenders in the community can be held in the home (e.g., for family interviews) or in public places where other people are somewhat nearby, but in a way that participant answers to survey or interview questions can be private. That is, the study participant must feel that answers are private and only heard by the researcher. For example, we have often met participants at fast food restaurants, public parks, or libraries but sat far enough away from others so that we were able to have a private conversation while remaining in view of other people. We also take precautions to protect ourselves from victimization, just as one might if going in public for other reasons. For example, we do not wear much jewelry, if any; we dress conservatively, park our cars in well-lit public areas, refrain from leaving electronics in our cars in view of passers-by, meet in public, and so on.

In sum, research with correctional populations—whether inside or outside of facilities—can cause physical or psychological harm that must be anticipated and mitigated prior to data collection. Some examples of potential harm while doing research with correctional populations and ways to reduce risk are presented below for avoiding physical harm to participants and researchers (box 4) as well as avoiding psychological harm to participants (box 5).

HOW TO AVOID COERCION OF PARTICIPANTS

To avoid coercion, researchers must take precautions when preparing to ask people to participate in the research. Participants *must not* feel pressured to participate by anyone, including researchers, correctional staff, other inmates, probationers, or parolees. This is critically important, because people under correctional control are, by definition, in a coercive situation because they are being forced by a court to be on probation, in a prison, or eventually released on parole. Federal research guidelines require that people participate in studies voluntarily, meaning they must not feel forced to participate (U.S. Department of

BOX 4. EXAMPLES OF POTENTIAL PHYSICAL HARM TO PARTICIPANTS AND RESEARCHERS AND WAYS TO REDUCE RISK

Examples of potential physical harm	Ways to reduce risk
By providing information about sensitive topics (e.g., criminal behavior), offenders may be subjected to harm from other offenders or formal sanctions by the institution or probation/parole officer or even face prosecution	• Gather anonymous data unless it will be necessary to follow-up with the participants at a later date (e.g., requiring participant confidentiality instead). • Avoid collecting identifying information, especially with regard to self-reported crimes (specific dates, names of people involved, etc.). • Avoid using signed informed consent forms if possible. If not possible, immediately separate consent forms from data collection forms and keep them separated in research files. Use unique identifying codes to indicate participants. Keep only one encrypted, password-protected file indicating which code matches which participant on an encrypted computer and in a locked cabinet.
Offenders could threaten other offenders against participating in the research (e.g., gang members may threaten other members to prevent them from participating)	• Terminate research or move research to other facilities/units where inmates will not be at as much risk. • Make the research project title vague to avoid too much unnecessary attention. • Consider all of the privacy protections noted above, and ensure that participants and others are aware that these precautions are being taken.

Offenders could use researcher-provided instruments (e.g., staples, pencils, pens) to harm themselves, correctional officers, researchers, or others	• Consider having the researchers fill out the form for survey/interview questions. • Consider providing golf pencils or flexible pens made for correctional populations instead of regular pens or full-size pencils. • Use as few (if any) staples as possible. • Do not use paper clips. • Employ a system for distributing and collecting materials to offenders (e.g., hand a writing instrument to each participant rather than allow participants to reach into a container themselves to obtain more than one, and count them before and after administration of surveys but before participants leave the area). • Inform participants of the system for distributing and collecting materials so they are aware that all materials must be returned. • Secure extra research materials away from offenders.
Offenders could use their bodies (e.g., fists) or institution-provided instruments (e.g., food trays or personal belongings) to harm themselves, correctional officers, researchers, or others	• Discuss personal safety concerns with correctional or program staff to create a safety plan (e.g., asking an officer or staff member to be present, carrying a "man down" pager). • Maintain a safe physical distance from offenders. • Consider avoiding high-risk facilities/units (e.g., maximum-security, solitary confinement, disciplinary units). • Limit the number of offenders in proximity to researchers at one time. • Use the "buddy system" (e.g., multiple researchers present during data collection). • Be aware of surroundings and suspicious behavior. • Terminate research and vacate area if necessary (e.g., trust your instincts).

BOX 5. EXAMPLES OF POTENTIAL PSYCHOLOGICAL HARM TO OFFENDERS AND WAYS TO REDUCE RISK

Examples of potential psychological harm	Ways to reduce risk
Researchers' sensitive questions could provoke negative thoughts and feelings for participants	• Explain any risk prior to participation. • Explain that participants can withdraw for any reason at any time (e.g., informed consent). • Provide resources for participants who experience negative thoughts/feelings (e.g., refer to institutional counselor or have a referral sheet for free counseling services if participants are not incarcerated).
Correctional or program staff could harass participants using verbal or nonverbal methods (e.g., In one of our experiences, a correctional officer shined flashlights on participants and gave participants "looks")	• Consider politely asking correctional officers or program staff to stop communicating/interacting with participants so they may concentrate on the research questions. Make the request privately so offenders cannot hear the request to avoid a power struggle with officers. • Consider temporarily or permanently terminating the data collection session. • Consider informing correctional or program administrators and requesting to conduct research in units supervised by other correctional officers or in the same units but on different shifts.

BOX 6. EXAMPLES OF POTENTIALLY COERCIVE SITUATIONS AND WAYS TO AVOID COERCION

Potentially coercive situations	Ways to avoid coercion
Researchers may inadvertently make it difficult for offenders by creating problems for nonparticipation	• Consider moving study participants to a private location to participate instead of requiring nonparticipants to move locations so that nonparticipants do not perceive negativity from prison staff for deciding not to participate. • Also, consider implementing a system where those who agree to participate remain in the research area for the same amount of time as those who decline, so institutional staff are unable to discern who did and did not participate in the study. • Reduce potential impositions on correctional officers or program staff who must relocate nonparticipants (e.g., conduct research in one separate area of the day room instead of asking staff to relocate offenders). Offenders may feel pressured to participate to avoid creating extra work for officers. Offenders might believe correctional officers will "retaliate" against inmates for creating extra work. • Reduce the number of correctional officers or program personnel involved in the identification of potential participants and in the actual moving of offenders. • Meet and/or interview probationers or parolees at public locations (for safety) comfortable for both the researchers and participant but outside of the probation and parole offices, where officers would be aware of who participates.

(continued)

BOX 6. *(continued)*

Officers/staff may do or say things that could inadvertently coerce offenders to participate	• Politely correct officers or program staff (either privately or publicly, depending upon the situation). For example, in one of our experiences, an officer asked a group of inmates "Who is going to participate in *my* survey?" Our research team quickly clarified in a jovial manner: "Just to be clear, this is *my* survey and the officer does not care one way or another if you participate." Reminding offenders about informed consent procedures is key to safeguarding informed consent and reducing coercion.
Offering too much incentive for participation could coerce offenders to participate	• The size of the incentive, if any, should match participants' time/effort and should not be so large that it becomes coercive, meaning potential respondents find it hard to decline. • Typical incentives for incarcerated participants are snacks/canteen/commissary items or a nominal monetary amount deposited into the inmate account (e.g., $10 or so). Similar incentives can be given to people under correctional control in the community. For juveniles, parental consent may be necessary for youths' participation and parents might approve or disapprove of their children receiving incentives, such as money or snacks. We had a situation, for example, where a parent requested that the incentive be given to the parent so the youth would not spend it on things they did not allow. The IRB will review incentives for possible coercion.
Administrators and lead staff may inadvertently pressure line staff to participate	• Researchers should introduce and administer the research materials, if possible, to avoid management involvement.

Health and Human Services n.d.). Box 6 features examples of potentially coercive situations and ways to avoid coercion.

Additionally, participants should not perceive themselves or others as being singled out for participation. This may occur if participants are randomly selected for participation or selected for participation based on some particular quality or characteristic (e.g., gang affiliation, type of criminal offense, race). It is possible that other offenders may incorrectly believe the selected offenders are not actually participating in research but are acting as "snitches" (informants) for correctional staff. It is important (and required by IRB) to communicate to the target population the reason for their selection to avoid misconceptions or coercion. Another option is to make the initial invitation as generic as possible for potential participants and then provide more specific information as part of the informed consent process. Although IRB approval requires participants be informed about why they were selected, there may be more appropriate and discreet times to provide this information (e.g., in private away from the general correctional population, in cases where the offender is in a facility). As discussed below, if any deception is used, then participants must be debriefed afterward.

There are numerous ways to encourage voluntary participation from correctional populations, including the following.

- ✓ Be respectful and polite, make eye contact, and speak normally.
- ✓ Introduce yourself and explain in plain terms the purpose of the research. That is, do not use academic jargon.
- ✓ Emphasize the importance of their participation (e.g., why should they care and what will happen if they participate).

✓ Ensure that the target population understands they have a choice whether to participate or not.

✓ Explain that researchers are not at all associated with the correctional institution or correctional system and that correctional or program staff will not see or touch any of the survey/interview materials. Rather, explain to the target population that aggregate data without any names may be provided to the facility, which presents results for the group as a whole. If the researcher works for the correctional system (not the institution), then they should clearly communicate how participants are protected.

✓ Offer an incentive for participants, if funds and correctional facilities permit. However, paying youths for their participation, although we have done it, can also require special consideration. In some cases parents asked us not to give their children cash, because they were concerned that the youths would spend it on something illegal. Depending on the situation and the agreement with the parents and IRB, researchers may choose to respond by not paying a particular child at all, by giving the youth a gift card instead, or by signing the cash over to the parents.

HOW TO PROTECT PARTICIPANTS' IDENTITIES

Protecting participants' identities is critical. Researchers can protect identities by promising either anonymity or confidentiality.

• *Anonymity*: The identity of participants is unknown to the researcher (e.g., name, employee number, or inmate ID number). This is the preferred option if no follow-up is necessary given that participants may be more likely to answer sensitive questions truthfully. Also, researchers may be able to avoid potential problems if the identities of participants become of interest to others (see "Summary of Ways to Increase Protection o Participant Identities" below); however, this is easiest in studies where there is only one data collection point (i.e., surveys are administered at one date and time). That is, in studies where researchers return multiple times to collect data, researchers need a plan to make sure that the same participant does not respond twice, such as a self-generated identification number (e.g., day of birth + number of siblings + number of children)

- *Confidentiality:* The researcher knows the identity of participants but promises not to disclose the identity to others, in reports, and so on unless required to do so by law. This type of protection is often necessary when future contact with the participant will be necessary (e.g., follow-up interviews or surveys) or when their interview data will be matched with their official records or other data sources (e.g., such as educational attendance or employment).

Despite researchers' best efforts to protect participants' identities, some particularly skeptical participants may incorrectly believe that researchers have the capability to identify participants using some sophisticated technology, such as fingerprint analysis (e.g., using fingerprints from the surveys they complete). On projects where we did not collect the participants' identities, we were (infrequently) presented with questions about anonymity. We assured participants that we possessed neither the equipment nor the motivation to identify them, and we reiterated that participation was anonymous and voluntary. Of course, every situation is different, and we recommend readers use common sense when deciding how to respond. In some instances, spending more time detailing the provisions outlined by the IRB or offering reasonable accommodation will be necessary to alleviate any potential concerns (e.g., wipe fingerprints from a computer used by participants). In other cases, as in the situation we encountered (mentioned above), the large number of participants or the needs of participants may necessitate a more streamlined assurance about their confidentiality/anonymity. In other words, some situations may not require a lengthy repetition of the IRB protocol. Researchers will need to make instant assessments and decisions about how to handle situations such as these most appropriately, honestly, and respectfully.

To ensure participants' anonymity in our Florida jail study, we did not collect signed informed consent forms from participants or request any identifying information (e.g., name or inmate identification number) on the survey. As part of the informed consent process, we emphasized several key aspects of the project to avoid any coercion. For example, before beginning data collection, we placed great emphasis on introducing ourselves as university researchers who were in no way associated with the jail. We further explained that the jail and the correctional officers did not care whether or not they participated. Participants were clearly informed that there were no benefits for participating (other than to help us understand their lives) and no penalties for not participating. We also explained that participation was voluntary and that participants could stop participating at any time or skip questions for any reason. Much like reviewing the details of a course syllabus to students on the first day of class, it can be tempting for researchers to gloss over these critically important, foundational details. However, we strongly encourage researchers to clearly, slowly, and deliberately communicate the content of the informed consent.

In other studies, where we provided confidentiality rather than anonymity due to the need to collect data from respondents at a later date or to match their interview or survey results with other records (e.g., in the evaluation of the SOCP and the Florida FCBDTI study mentioned in previous chapters), we used other procedures. For example, as noted above, we took extra precautions to ensure the identifiers were not ever stored with the individual data, including immediately after the data collection (e.g., cover sheets were separated from data immediately and transported in different boxes or envelopes) or at any time later. We also locked the crosswalk (the file that lists the study identification number with the identifier) for the study and identifiers away in one file in a cabinet (including any flash drive files) and did not keep electronic copies on our computers. Data files used to run analysis did not include any identifiers, including any personal information, inmate or probation case numbers, and so on. It is also useful to destroy the paper files once electronic data files are created and include all the information on the hard copies. It is also common practice for participants to provide approval or disapproval for any additional data that will be collected so the participants have the power to determine which data sources they approve of.

Researchers' data from offenders about crimes may become of interest to other people, including law enforcement agencies. This has occasionally resulted in legal action where researchers are requested—or even subpoenaed—to reveal confidential information. The party requesting the information may believe the researcher possesses data regarding threats to public safety, whereas the researcher may believe providing the data is a violation of confidentiality and academic freedom. Although rare, some researchers have had to decide whether to comply with legal requests for data or protect the identity of participants.[1] Box 7 features this dilemma faced by Rick Scarce.

Summary of Ways to Increase Protection of Participant Identities

✓ Keep identities of participants anonymous to the researcher, if possible.

✓ Avoid asking participants to sign the informed consent form so their names cannot be located on this form. If consent forms are signed, keep them separate from the data collection instruments (e.g., in different envelopes), including immediately following data collection (e.g., while at the facility or other data collection site).

✓ If participants' identities are known, assign a unique study identifier to match survey/interview responses to official records in study data files.

✓ Keep any keys or files that link names to unique identifiers in a private, locked location with restricted access.

✓ Destroy participants' personal identifiers as soon as possible. While this can be especially problematic for longitudinal research designed to track people after release from prison or correctional control, keeping identifiers safe is especially important.

1. Issues related to protecting participants' identities (where the researcher in these instances has done nothing wrong) are distinct from liability, where researchers have not followed approved IRB protocol (e.g., using data for another purpose that harms subjects).

BOX 7. THE CASE OF RICK SCARCE'S ETHICAL DILEMMA

When Rick Scarce was a graduate student at Washington State University his interviews with an animal rights activist became of interest to law enforcement during a criminal investigation. As part of his dissertation research, Scarce conducted interviews with several animal rights activists. Soon after the interviews, a fire was set to animal research facilities on campus. Law enforcement identified one of Scarce's participants as a suspect in the arson and requested that Scarce breach confidentiality by answering questions and providing transcripts from the interviews with the suspect. As a result of his refusal to testify to a federal grand jury, Scarce was convicted of contempt of court and incarcerated in jail for five months. In his book *Contempt of Court* (2005), Scarce describes the many personal and professional consequences he faced in an effort to preserve his research integrity. Unfortunate situations like this are rare; yet, these situations often encourage researchers to consider the extent to which they are willing to protect their research participants. While preventing any potential legal liability may be impossible, researchers would benefit by thinking about ways to keep inmates' identities anonymous/confidential in an effort to reduce the likelihood of these situations. In addition, universities can often provide legal advice if IRB procedures were followed. In the event that a researcher is sued, some universities may offer legal counsel if the project was IRB approved. Researchers may wish to inquire about this at their institution.

PARENTAL CONSENT/ASSENT: GAINING
PERMISSION AND MAINTAINING ACCESS
TO CONDUCT RESEARCH ON JUVENILE
CORRECTIONAL POPULATIONS

Juveniles involved in the correctional system represent a unique study population, because they have two characteristics that pose challenges for researchers and classify them as a vulnerable group in terms of research. First, if the youth are incarcerated, researchers must be concerned about whether any agreement to participate in research is truly voluntary and not coerced (see 45 CFR §46.302, Protection of Human Subjects). In addition, they are generally under eighteen years old, or legally a minor, meaning that they also receive extra protections as subjects of research. Ethics researchers worry that children, due to their age, lack of emotional and intellectual maturity, and their susceptibility to adult influence may not be competent to provide consent, meaning to "choose autonomously for oneself" whether it is in their best interests to participate in the research (Miller, Drotar, and Kodish 2004, 256). Research has shown that children's ability to understand the implications of informed consent generally increases with age, but this increase in understanding depends on context of the study and is true for some details of research and not others. That is, the research studies looking at various aspects of consent for youths are mixed on whether age matters (Miller, Drotar, and Kodish 2004). One recent study of the MacArthur Competence Assessment Tool for Clinical Research, however, found that competence to participate in research was probable around ten or eleven years old (Hein et al. 2014).

Because of these concerns about youths' ability to understand what they are getting into, juveniles can only give "assent" to participate in research, which is a term used to differentiate a child's willingness to participate from a "legally valid authorization" to conduct research on them (Miller, Drotar, and Kodish 2004, 256). For research on children to ensue, permission or consent must generally be attained from parents or legal guardians (48 FR 918, §46.408; U.S. Department of Health and Human Services 1979). Yet, even this procedure has raised some concerns among researchers if studies seek only parental permission, because it can lead to situations in which the youths' feelings are ignored (e.g., see Coyne 2010). Over time, researchers have come to see informed consent with children as an interactive process, looking at youths' individual experiences and ability to understand the circumstances of research (Alderson 2007).

Consequently, in the design of any study involving youths under correctional control, there should be multiple layers of permission/consent and assent. Importantly, obtaining agreement (e.g., from the agency or administrators) is different from obtaining consent/assent (e.g., from parents and youth). It is not enough to get permission of the facility or probation officer, although this is necessary, and then ask the child if he/she would like to talk to you. Rather, researchers typically must obtain agreement from the agency, and consent/assent from one or more parents and the child. Particularly with minimal risk protocols, consent is usually not required from both parents.

For example, in our study evaluating faith-based programming among youths in incarcerated in Florida, we put into the study design multiple points where consent/assent was to occur for data collection to proceed. First, when a youth was being considered for residential placement—at a commitment hearing—both the parent and youth were asked to sign a general informed consent indicating that they *may* be asked to participate in a study (with actual consents signed later). By signing this form, both were agreeing to participate in a faith-based program that was part of a study if chosen to be placed in one of these facilities (see appendix F).[2] If they did not want to participate in a faith-based program, they could choose not to sign the consent and would be placed in a non-faith-based facility. The research team did not contact these individuals. However, this was often a tense meeting, as youths and parents were often stressed about the commitment hearing itself. After all, many of the youths there were being removed from their homes to be placed in a facility. So, we did continue to garner consent at different points in the study. For example, we had planned to interview youths at least two times (near the beginning of the program and at twelve months postcommitment). At each interview we also had the youths sign an assent form (which was called re-consent form in the study) to indicate that they were still willing to participate in the study (see appendix G). We also were careful to ensure verbally that they understood in layperson terms what would be happening and to answer any questions, reiterating that they could stop at any time if they were uncomfortable. Because these assent forms included youth identifiers (their names), they were immediately separated from the data collection instruments and were kept separately in a locked filing cabinet to maintain security. In addition, because the youths were wards of the court at the time, we were not required to get parental consent for subsequent interviews, if we had obtained it already. Of course, at any time, the

2. The consent forms for the FCBDTI were primarily designed by Dr. Lonn Lanza-Kaduce, another principal investigator on the FCBDTI project. For more information on the FCBDTI, please refer to the project final report (Lane et al. 2009).

youths could decline participation without any penalty from us or the facility.

In another project of ours called the SOCP, the program was composed of several agencies including probation, mental health, alcohol and drug abuse counselors, mentors, and more. Therefore, this project itself initially had youths and their families sign a waiver to allow for the release of information about their cases across agencies. The evaluation team was included in this initial release, which generally allowed us access to the youths' official records from these agencies. However, to be safe in terms of access to official records and to conduct interviews with the youths, we obtained both parental consent and youth assent that were specific to the study itself (see appendix H for an example of a form to obtain both parental consent and youth assent).

Although our examples document consent using in-person procedures, it is possible to gain parental consent via alternative means. If, for example, potential study participants are identified in an incarcerated setting and parents are not easily accessible, an IRB may allow parental consent via telephone, with the process recorded.

DECEPTION AND DISCLOSURE

Is Deception in the Name of Science Ethical?

Whether deception is ethical is a difficult question to answer given that much depends upon on researchers' consideration of several important questions (see below) as well as IRB approval. Deception could involve deceiving participants about the identity of the researcher. Although it is uncommon for researchers to use deception, some relevant examples include: Goffman's (1961) classic research in *Asylums*, Erickson and Tewksbury's (2000) study of strip clubs where they posed as clients, and Goode's (1996a) posting of bogus personal advertisements. Certainly, using deception in social science is controversial (see, for example, Goode 1996b). Any form of deception must receive IRB and correctional facility approval and, once participants are debriefed, they must be given the option to have their data destroyed and removed from the study. When considering whether to deceive participants, researchers will inevitably grapple with several considerations:

- Do the potential problems outweigh the potential benefits associated with deception?
- Could ethical problems arise?
- Could the research be done as effectively without deception?
- Could deception do physical or emotional harm to participants or institutions?
- Could deception do harm to the researcher's professional reputation or the researcher's professional relationship with the institution?

If the answer to any of these questions is yes, then the ethical and responsible answer is likely to avoid deception. Although research with correctional populations does not have to be risk-free, the benefits of deception must outweigh risks, which is true for all research with any population. Researchers considering deception should consider the ethical principles outlined by the Belmont Report as mentioned earlier (e.g., respect for people, beneficence, and justice; see U.S. Department of Health and Human Services 1979).

BOX 8. EXAMPLE OF INCOMPLETE DISCLOSURE USED BY THE AUTHORS OF THIS BOOK

In their research with Florida jail inmates, Fox and Lane were primarily interested in gang membership and crime victimization, among a variety of other topics. The researchers were concerned that describing the survey to inmates as a survey about "gangs and victimization" would result in very few participants. Given that the survey contained numerous questions about a wide variety of other topics, the researchers received IRB and jail approval to tell inmates that the survey was about their personal characteristics, neighborhood, and crime (which broadly covered the specific topics of interest as well as other questions covered in the survey). Based on researchers' observations, this minor form of incomplete disclosure did not appear to negatively affect inmates. Debriefing was not necessary or required by the IRB given that participants were not deceived.

Incomplete Disclosure as an Alternative to Deception

Incomplete disclosure is the disclosure of some information and the withholding of other information. This may be a viable alternative to deception. As an example of incomplete disclosure, a study that focuses on socially undesirable behavior (e.g., deviant sexual behavior, gang activity, victimization) may downplay this focus if the survey/interview includes a variety of other questions (see box 8).

Disclosing to Participants Other Information Related
to the Research

Researchers may grapple with some decisions about what information to provide or withhold from participants about themselves and about the study:

- What personal information, if any, will researchers disclose to participants?
- Will researchers provide transcripts of the interviews to participants? What if participants request to see this information?
- What happens if participants disclose personally identifying information on anonymous surveys/ interviews?
- What if offenders say they are planning to hurt themselves or others?

Many of these questions are concerns for IRB and must be addressed during the IRB approval process. In our experiences, we sometimes provide personal information and sometimes not, although we do not ever provide much detail. For example, when conducting research with jail inmates, we chose not to provide personal information by politely "pleading the Fifth Amendment" to offenders who asked inappropriate personal questions. We made this decision because we found it to be effective to avoid potential pitfalls and series of frivolous questions that would detract from our professional purpose. In other cases, we shared some information, such as what school we worked at, how long we had been there, or what we did for fun (nonspecific). That is, we shared some information about ourselves without sharing details that might decrease our safety. Scholars might elect to share some personal information in an effort to build rapport with participants. For example, scholars might decide to share their own experiences related to the research (e.g., victim or ex-convict status) to gain rapport with participants; however, this could result in other problems (e.g., projecting one's own experiences or feelings on participants or participants may not explain their feelings/experiences by assuming the researcher shares similar feelings/experiences).

In the event that participants request copies of the data they provided (e.g., their own interview transcripts or survey responses) or reports that use their data, we recommend following IRB protocol. Making copies of this information can be logistically challenging, especially in correctional settings. And other people, including other offenders or correctional staff, could view the data—with or without participants' permission—which could have serious implications for confidentiality. Yet, it may be less problematic to provide copies of transcripts to probationers or parolees, because they may be better able to keep the transcript private. Researchers will need to use their judgment in these cases and follow IRB and state requirements.

In our experience, offenders occasionally volunteered their name and contact information despite our anonymous research. We refused any pieces of paper with contact information. We immediately removed and destroyed any identifying information that we discovered on anonymous surveys, and this also can be done with transcriptions of tape-recorded interviews.

There should be language in the informed consent regarding notification procedures to be taken if someone informs the researcher of plans to hurt themselves or others. Researchers should check their state's law and university's IRB policy prior to data collection. For example, states often require that researchers disclose if the respondents are planning to hurt themselves or others (Bureau of Justice Statistics 2001).

Ethics When Reporting Research Findings

While the following ethical principles are important for reporting any research, including noncorrectional populations, these tips are critical for researchers who work with correctional institutions:

- Provide correctional administrators with at least a brief summary report void of academic jargon and technical statistical models to maintain positive professional relationships.
- Allow participating agencies the ability to comment/ review drafts.[3]
- Acknowledge contributors in publications (e.g., participants while maintaining confidentiality/anonymity, agency administrators, correctional institutions, funding agencies, and research assistants).
- Ensure anonymity of participants and correctional/ program staff and facilities in reports (unless they want to be named).
- Attempt to publish the findings in highly visible outlets to advance science.

Collaborating with correctional agencies and studying correctional populations often means that researchers are tackling

3. Publication of project findings can depend upon grant and contract language. For this reason, we recommend that if work is done under contract/ grant, researchers work out in advance any requirements and restrictions for publication.

important issues that have real implications for people. For example, correctional jobs may be cut if an evaluation returns negative results for a correctional program. A researcher's casual remark that is overheard by those in authority about difficulties working with certain correctional staff or offenders can have serious punitive implications for the staff member or offenders. Professionalism, tact, and honesty are valuable qualities that can help researchers remain ethical when reporting (verbally or in writing) their research findings.

ADVICE FOR APPLYING FOR APPROVAL FROM UNIVERSITY AND CORRECTIONAL IRBS

University and correctional IRBs will want to see that researchers have anticipated and accounted for the ethical considerations we have discussed. Anticipating and accounting for ethical considerations will demonstrate to IRBs and correctional agencies that the researchers are knowledgeable about these important and practical issues, which will increase the likelihood of obtaining approval to conduct the research. The following may not be exhaustive lists of important information to include in the IRB materials, and readers are encouraged to carefully follow the guidelines and any template language specified in their own IRB.

Examples of What to Include in the IRB Informed Consent Form

*Note: this form should be very concise (preferably one page) to avoid overwhelming participants and to improve the chances they will read the document. (See appendices F, G, and H for examples.)

✓ Project title

✓ Purpose of the study (preferably one sentence)

✓ What participants will be asked to do

✓ Approximate length of time participation will take

✓ Confidentiality/anonymity

✓ Incentive, if any

✓ Voluntary participation

✓ Researchers' contact information (e.g., name, university address, phone number, e-mail address)

✓ University IRB contact information

✓ Participation agreement (e.g., instruct participants to either sign/do not sign document)

✓ Notify participants that they may keep a copy of the informed consent

Examples of Information to Include in the IRB Application/Protocol

*Note: this form should be as detailed as possible to improve the chances that the IRB application will be approved. (See appendix I for example.)

✓ Project title

✓ Researchers' information (e.g., name, university ID number, address, phone number, e-mail address)

✓ Dates of proposed research (e.g., start and completion dates)

✓ Funding sources, if any

✓ Scientific purpose of the study (e.g., research aims, research questions, potential policy implications)

✓ Methodology (e.g., clearly explain the procedures including sampling, nature of the survey/interview questions, research setting, materials to be used)

✓ Potential benefits and risks to participants, and ways to minimize the risks

✓ Recruiting procedure for participants

✓ Informed consent process (e.g., voluntary participation, right to withdraw without penalty, anonymity/confidentiality, and incentives, if any)

✓ The finalized survey/interview questions, including response options

✓ How data will be safeguarded

Tips to Improve the Chances of Receiving University and Correctional IRB Approval

✓ Explain how the research will benefit the correctional agency/program and/or participants.

✓ Obtain letter of support from institution on institution letterhead, and offer to write a sample letter that the agency can modify (see appendix A, discussed earlier, for sample letter).

✓ Become familiar with university and correctional IRB websites to learn about deadlines, correct forms to use, and required information.

✓ Budget extra time and plan for full board (rather than expedited) IRB review, which can take a few months.

✓ Attend IRB meetings, if possible, to be available to answer questions and address problems that arise.

✓ Proofread your materials to ensure the final submission is free from errors and omissions.

✓ Request that faculty supervisor or research partners review final (proofread) submission, if applicable.

While IRBs are interested in standard information pertaining to ethical data collection, IRBs are all unique. Projects that are approved by one IRB may not be by another. Importantly, the IRB protocol and informed consent should clearly outline the proposed project and address all ethical concerns. See Stone (2004) for a comprehensive historical overview of the ethical issues of researching inmates. For additional IRB guidelines for researching correctional populations, see the U.S. Department of Health and Human Services (2003) and the National Institutes of Health (2011b).

CONCLUSION

Because the most important aspect of any research project is to reduce unnecessary harm and to protect participants' rights, we highlighted in this chapter key ways to help researchers plan for a smooth and safe research design. Avoiding coercion is particularly important among correctional populations given the nature of total institutions and the power dynamics at play (e.g., between offender and staff and between staff and top administrators). Also, researchers should take extreme care to ensure that all aspects of the informed consent process are judiciously followed.

The next chapter offers essential "nuts and bolts" recommendations based on the realities of collecting data from correctional populations. Among other topics, we discuss how to recruit and train research assistants, what to wear to collect the data, important things to consider before data collection, how to handle uncomfortable situations, ideas for keeping records organized, and pitfalls to avoid. The following chapter concludes this book and serves as a practical roadmap for successfully navigating the many moving parts that are inevitably part of doing research with correctional populations.

CHAPTER FIVE

Logistics of Doing Research with Correctional Populations

The making of a successful academic scholar is some combination of nature and nurture. The same is true for those scholars who successfully navigate research with correctional populations. We begin this chapter by identifying the key qualifications and professional skills (e.g., the nurtured or learned qualities), as well as personal characteristics (e.g., one's natural or chosen qualities), which we feel are important for successful research with correctional populations.

*Important Professional Skills/Qualifications for
Conducting Research with Correctional Populations*

- Personal experience with correctional populations and/or gained knowledge of these groups through reading of prior studies conducted in correctional settings. Reading of personal accounts by academics, practitioners, or correctional clients may also be useful. These sources provide background knowledge but also may attune the researcher to relevant information useful to the study at hand (e.g., important questions to ask, hurdles to anticipate, and issues to navigate, including political ones). This includes a basic understanding of the way the justice system operates (e.g., arrest, prosecution, sentencing, sanctions).

• A working knowledge (e.g., from a textbook, class, and/or the literature) or personal experience with the type of data collection method to be used in the project (e.g., survey, interview, focus group). Dedicated training on the specifics of sampling, instrument construction, field research, etc. is very useful. Training can occur in dedicated methods courses or in specialty workshops, such as those taught at the Interuniversity Consortium for Political and Social Research or the annual American Society of Criminology conference's pre-meeting workshops.

• Guidance and mentoring from others more knowledgeable in working with the chosen data collection methods, correctional populations, and field research. This could be one person with all these qualities or a group of mentors (e.g., a carefully selected dissertation committee, group of colleagues, or practitioners).

*Important Personal Qualities for Conducting Research
with Correctional Populations*

• Patience. As we highlight throughout this chapter and this book, research with correctional populations is very time consuming and requires an immense amount of patience on the part of the researcher. Gaining access, dealing with delays, and managing relationships with staff and offenders takes time and involves a lot of waiting. Researchers who approach these situations with unrealistic expectations regarding time run the risk of (directly or indirectly) conveying a negative attitude that destroys rapport and impedes data collection.

- Persistence. Being patient does not mean being passive. Instead, persistence—in a polite, friendly, and respectful manner—is essential for navigating research with correctional populations. In our experience, our phone calls and e-mails to correctional administrators often went unreturned. We were often diligent and proactive in our pursuit to gain access, overcome scheduling conflicts, think creatively about problem solving, and communicate with people who had different priorities than us. With that in mind, we also respected when correctional facilities or people with the appropriate authority told us "no."

- Ability to maintain poise and professionalism in stressful or uncomfortable situations. Encountering correctional populations and facilities means stepping out of one's comfort zone. Researchers might see or hear people do or say unprofessional, inappropriate, or troubling things (see below for a discussion on this topic). To maintain professionalism and rapport with correctional agencies and participants, it is essential for researchers to remain calm in all situations. Follow the lead of the correctional staff when situations arise (e.g., lockdowns). When unexpected situations occur, take a moment to think first, then speak and take action.

- Genuine interest in and excitement about researching correctional populations. We have found that researchers and assistants who are passionate about doing correctional research have the most success and receive the most enjoyment from their efforts.

Selecting and Training Research Assistants

Selecting and training research assistants to do research with correctional populations are other challenges many researchers face. In our experience, research assistants who were most excited about the project made for the most reliable, dependable, and helpful team members. We also found that the most successful methods of advertising for research assistants (both graduate and undergraduate students) are via word of mouth (especially personal recruitment of top students) and verbal announcements during class. Other ways to find research assistants may involve displaying flyers on campus, sending e-mails to prospective assistants, or formally posting an advertisement via human resources. We have also had success using an application for prospective research assistants to complete (see appendix J for an example research assistant application).

Once the pool of eligible applicants has been vetted, we recommend meeting with candidates individually to assess the skills and personal characteristics that are most important for your research. The following interview questions may be useful to discuss during this initial meeting.

BOX 9. THINGS TO CONSIDER: RESEARCHERS' GENDER, RACE/ETHNICITY, AGE, SEXUALITY, ETC.

Researchers' and research assistants' demographics may be important to consider, especially if they are interacting with participants. Because we, as the authors of this book, are all women, our experiences are necessarily shaped in part by our gender, among other qualities. While it is certainly possible for men to have similar or different experiences as ours, we believe some personal qualities are much more critical and impactful on participants than gender. For example, we believe the so-called feminine qualities of being kind, cheerful, and understanding of others (Spence and Buckner 2000) that we exhibited with participants were more influential than our being female. It may be useful to select research assistants who may bring needed skills and/or expertise to the project. On one project, one of us selected a particularly capable and motivated bilingual female undergraduate student to help collect data from men and women in jail. This student was fluent in Spanish, and she not only assisted with creating the Spanish version of the survey instrument, but she also made the announcement and administered the survey in Spanish to those inmates who preferred to take the survey in that language. On another project, one of us interviewed prison inmates with the assistance of a male undergraduate student (who exhibited personal qualities of kindness, friendliness, and acceptance) and who showed the ability to develop rapport with male inmates. In other situations, we worked with a wide variety of male and female research assistants of a variety of races/ethnicities (but all were young, given the average age of the university population), and these students primarily helped with entering data. We strongly encourage researchers to consider the advantages offered by the different demographics of their research assistants (see also the literature on the effects of interviewers' characteristics, including gender, race, age, etc.; Davis et al. 2010).

Example Interview Questions for Selecting Research Assistants

- This project will involve your help with the following tasks [insert description here]. The project is expected to last [insert months/years], so I am looking for research assistants who can make this kind of long-term commitment to the project. Will your school and work schedules allow for you to work on the project that long? What days/times are you available? How many months/semesters/quarters are you available?

- Do you have reliable transportation for traveling to the correctional facility?

- What makes you interested in (or excited about) this research project?

- What prior coursework have you completed (e.g., methodology or statistics courses)?

- What is your prior experience working on research projects? What is your prior experience working on projects that are governed by an internal research board (human subjects)? While prior experience is ideal, we often had great success working with research assistants with no prior research experience, when we provided strong training.

- Are you certified by the Collaborative Institutional Training Initiative (CITI)?

- What aspects of the research process do you have experience with? E.g., proposal writing, design and instrument development, recruitment, administration of surveys, interviews, data cleaning and management, analysis and report writing.

- Can you describe your writing skills? May I see a writing sample?

- The correctional facility will require that you pass a background check, meaning they check your criminal record. Are you comfortable with this?

- As part of this project, you'll learn sensitive and private things about people. To protect people's privacy and the integrity of the project, it's important that you do not share information with others outside of the project. Are you able to do this?

When research assistants have been selected, we recommend a hands-on approach with frequent training, updates, check-ins, and communication. An initial training should be conducted where assistants practice these learned skills, especially if there will be a team of research assistants. Researchers may then select from the pool of research assistants who performed the best in the initial training. If research assistants will be collecting data from correctional populations, consider requiring them to go in pairs as this will make data collection more efficient and also may increase feelings of safety. This may be especially important if research assistants are meeting people outside of a correctional institution where there are no officers available to ensure researchers' safety. Similar to the safety concerns for lead researchers themselves as discussed in an earlier section, it is also important to think about research assistants' safety when coordinating a meeting place with participants; e.g., meet participants in public places, do not divulge their own cell phone numbers, addresses, or social media information, and avoid going to unsafe places (high crime/drug dealing areas or gang hangouts). We sometimes get a dedicated disposable "burner" phone to use for research projects, so that we are always available, but our own phone numbers remain private. The adage "safety first" is especially important to keep in mind at all stages of data collection.

If research assistants will be transcribing interviews or entering survey data into statistical packages, ensure there is a unique number or code assigned to each research assistant that is entered for each and every case they record in the file (i.e., include it as a variable in the dataset). We found this practice helpful when assessing the productivity and accuracy of each research assistant. In addition, it is useful to know who entered the data, should questions arise about information entered (e.g., unusual codes or oddly missing data). Some assistants may be better interviewers (e.g., ask more in-depth follow-up questions) or better at recording data than others, and this may affect results. In addition to data on participants, it is important to have information on methods issues that may affect results. We often collect information on data collector, date of data collection, start and end time, location of data collection, and other contextual variables that may matter. For example, we note if the participant appeared to be paying attention or on drugs, or if there were distractions that interrupted data collection.

We also recommend creating a detailed data file for data entry that contains all of the variable names and coding labels in the file. The complete data file should be prepared before giving the data file to the assistants for data entry (meaning variable names and value labels for codes, etc.). Having detailed description of the variable names in the data file helps assistants know what codes to use if they forget. In addition, it is useful to create a data entry codebook, with complete instructions on how to enter the data into the statistical data file. This could be available to assistants in hard copy and/or in PDF format, so they can easily refer to the codebook while entering data.

It might be wise also to have the assistants save the data file with their initials and the date on the end each time it is edited to prevent accidental loss of data files and data. That is, if one person makes a mistake and loses data or a file is corrupted, the file from the day before should remain intact. This will mean that should something go wrong with the data file, only one day's worth of work will be lost rather than multiple days' worth. We sometimes also make multiple copies of the original data template file and give one to each research assistant, merging the data files from each assistant at consistent intervals ourselves (e.g., after every fifty surveys are entered in to each file or at the end of the semester). Of course, these multiple files must not be floating around on multiple unsecured servers. In other words, the protections and requirements outlined by the institutional review board (IRB) must still be followed. These are just simple strategies to allow regular checks on data entry and minimize crises if mistakes are made.

For qualitative data, it is also a good strategy to have one research assistant type the original transcription and then another listen to the voice recording to double check the accuracy of the

1. Filename on Voice File:	
2. Date(s) and Times Transcribed:	
3. Filename for Transcription:	
4. Transcriber Name:	
5. Checker Name:	
6. Date Transcription Checked:	

Figure 3. Transcription template. Source: Authors

originally transcribed words, each putting their initials at the end of the files they edit. Assistants should be told the importance of transcribing verbatim, including slang, curse words, and so forth, to ensure the researchers can accurately portray the attitudes and beliefs of respondents in their write-ups. We have often provided a template at the top of the form in which they enter the qualitative data transcriptions, so that the transcription data file itself includes the information about how the data were recorded. Figure 3, for example, can be at the top of each file to ensure that researchers know details for each transcription as they analyze them. We also recommend keeping an Excel file for qualitative data with a log of progress on each data file, including who has what transcription/audio recording, when they received it, when it was returned, who checked it, when, and so on.

Once research assistants have been selected, you might consider giving or loaning them a copy of this book so that they may learn from our experiences. Assistants should also read and agree to the conditions and practices laid out in the IRB protocol. Some universities even have online IRB training modules for research assistants, and sometimes these are required rather than optional. Of course, assistants need to be added to the IRB if they are working with identified data or performing any of the research tasks, including recruiting and consenting participants.

APPROPRIATE ATTIRE FOR MEN AND WOMEN

Correctional agencies and especially facilities are notorious for having rigid rules, often for good reason, and this typically includes specific instructions for visitor (read: researcher) attire. Be sure to ask in advance for the agency's dress code policy. During meetings with correctional staff and gatekeepers, we recommend business attire (e.g., suit and jacket or sports coat for men and women, or if not a suit, other professional clothing) to establish and maintain professional first impressions.

Inside correctional institutions we dressed in business casual (e.g., dress pants and button-down shirt or blouse, or slacks and collared shirt for men). Given the amount of necessary standing and walking through correctional institutions, we avoided high heels and wore comfortable, closed-toe shoes. We also found it useful to avoid particularly bright or distracting colors, because we were already highly visible given our "outsider" status. Each correctional facility will have their own set of specific rules that visitors (including researchers) must follow. For example, the guidelines for visitors of California prisons provides a specific list of items to avoid, including clothing with metal buttons and bras with underwire (because they may not clear a metal detector), camouflage clothing, hats, and hairpieces, wigs, or other headpieces (unless prior approval is granted) (California Department of Corrections and Rehabilitation n.d.). In Florida, people visiting prisons are not permitted to wear such things as ripped jeans, shorts, sandals, and see-through or revealing clothing, and they are prohibited from bringing in things that can be contraband inside (e.g., cell phones, bottle openers—like those often on key chains, and pocket knives). We regularly take students on tours of local prisons, for example, and students have been turned away for showing too much cleavage or their midriff. It is also typically very important to have official state identification (e.g., driver's license or identification card) to enter a prison as a visitor. Prisons may also require preclearance background checks before entry, and the reason for declined clearance due to the background check may not be given (but can include issues such as current or past criminal justice status).

The same recommendations apply to meeting with people who work in community corrections or people on probation or parole. It is important to look professional and dress conservatively. Unique personal styles are not necessarily appropriate in correctional settings, because correctional venues tend to be conservative places and unique personal styles sometimes imply philosophies or opinions of researchers. While we all are entitled to our own styles and opinions, it is important that participants perceive researchers as neutral so they feel freer to be open about their own attitudes and beliefs. For example, one of us sometimes wears "hippie" skirts, but would never do so in a research setting, because some system personnel might perceive that it implies certain beliefs and might not share their own if considered contrary.

Specific Tips for Men and Women on How to Dress in Correctional Settings

- Avoid tight-fitting or revealing clothing (e.g., no visible midriffs or cleavage, no short skirts, no low-cut shirts, no see-through material or clothes with stylish holes).
- Wear full-length pants with pockets for carrying approved items (e.g., lip balm, mints, or lozenges). Most facilities do not allow visitors to bring in bags or

cellphones. Car keys may be permitted or stored in a prison locker.

- Layers will be useful if the facility is extremely hot or cold (we experienced both extreme temperatures inside different units).

- Wear comfortable shoes for long periods of walking or standing (and expect to take them off to go through metal detectors).

- Minimize jewelry, although a wristwatch can be helpful, because cell phones often must be left outside in a locker or in one's car. Too much jewelry can be distracting and, for some, might imply class differences that could lead to less trust of the researcher. In addition, jewelry may create difficulty going through metal detectors, if this is a necessary step to enter the agency or facility.

The key point is that it is important to carefully consider choice of clothing. As noted, it is important to think about how those to whom you are talking will perceive you. Beyond the ultimate goal of ensuring safety of all involved, it is critically important that the participant trust the researcher, and clothing is one way in our culture that we convey messages about who we are and what we believe. One can rarely go wrong in correctional settings by dressing in a professional, conservative manner.

QUESTIONS TO DISCUSS WITH CORRECTIONAL STAFF PRIOR TO DATA COLLECTION

Before beginning data collection, we recommend communicating with correctional staff regarding a number of procedural issues, including the following.

General Questions

- What is the best way to contact the correctional organization to arrange research visits once data collection begins?

- How will the research team invite clients or staff to participate (e.g., as a group or individually and via announcement or conversation)?

- Where will participants participate (e.g., how will inmates be relocated, if necessary; or can probation and parole offices be used for interviews/surveys?)[1] If necessary, are there private areas in which to collect data?

- How will research materials be distributed and collected (for example, if data collection with staff or correctional clients occurs in a group setting or if staff or correctional clients are not available all at one time)?

- How will correctional staff be asked not to handle research materials that are completed by clients, both before and after the data are collected? What is the best way to convey the message to staff that this must be done by researchers?

- Is there a way to allow completed data forms (e.g., surveys) to be returned anonymously or confidentially (e.g., through prepaid postage envelopes provided by the researcher or a locked drop box at a facility, to which only the research team has access)?

1. Remember, that it is important here to ensure anonymity in terms of research participation. If possible, researchers may want other locations for data collection outside the correctional location. In addition, it is important to allow people to come to the research location and not disclose to others which people actually did or did not participate while there.

- What are the daily routines of the organization? What do researchers need to be aware of when conducting research (e.g., schedules, unusual events [scheduled or unscheduled], rules, staffing changes)?
- How can and should the research team request data (e.g., client or inmate records or statistics on the probation, parole, inmate, or juvenile population being examined)?
- Are there any particular clients or inmates who should be excluded in the research, and if so, why?[2]

Questions Specific to Correctional Institutions

- Who will escort the research team throughout the facility (name, title, shift times)?
- How will the escort call attention to the clients, and what will he/she say?
- Will correctional staff be inside the room during data collection? Ideally, staff would remain outside of the room or, if they must remain inside due to facility rules or safety concerns, then participant confidentiality must still be ensured.
- What type of security will be available to the research team?
- What types of research materials are allowed and what types are not (e.g., pens/pencils, survey or interview instruments, laptops, electronic tablets, voice recorders)? What are the procedures for checking materials at each visit?

---

2. It is typical, for example, for correctional organizations to exclude clients with mental health issues or extreme behavior problems, unless these groups are the specific focus of the research project.

Before data collection begins, it is important to think through the types of requests for data or materials you will need so that these documents or electronic versions can be obtained *before* leaving the facility or agency in the field. For example, researchers might need certain data to analyze response rates or to make comparisons between the sample and the population (e.g., population counts, demographic data, or offense data). It can be extremely difficult to obtain data or information after leaving the facility or agency, if one is not returning for another data collection session. In addition, counts in facilities and in facility locations vary by day and time of day, and it may be difficult to later determine the number of people in the room who were invited to participate at the time of data collection. Moreover, agency staff are busy, might transfer to a different unit, or may even retire. Even if staff promise to (and genuinely intend to) e-mail the information right away, it may not happen or the wrong information may be sent if there was a miscommunication about what data is requested. We recommend offering to wait while staff prepare the requested materials so that researchers ensure they have everything they need before leaving the facility. Or, in some cases, it is helpful to tell the staff ahead of time what type of information you will need, so they have time to prepare the information before your visit.

WHAT TO DO WHEN OFFENDERS ASK INAPPROPRIATE QUESTIONS OR BEHAVE INAPPROPRIATELY

Offenders have rarely asked us inappropriate questions. Some inappropriate questions that we were asked pertained to the type of perfume we wore, whether we had a partner/spouse, and requests for us to contact offenders' family members on their behalf. We declined requests and we did not answer personal questions (see the section "Deception and Disclosure" in chapter 4 for strategies we used to easily navigate uncomfortable questions).

In our experience, offenders rarely behaved inappropriately toward us. Occasionally, offenders have directed profane language and inappropriate comments at us. Infrequently, offenders masturbated in our presence. Our strategy was to ignore inappropriate behavior whenever possible or request that the behavior stop, and to terminate the participant's interview/survey if needed. It is understandable sometimes that incarcerated people may stare or flirt with people who enter facilities. Many have been incarcerated for years and have seen very few other people, especially people of the opposite sex, in street clothes during that time. We are not easily rattled, and we selected research assistants with this similar quality, so it was relatively easy to defuse uncomfortable situations by maintaining focus on the research and ignoring distractions. For example, in our jail study we did not make eye contact with or react in any way to inmates who engaged in inappropriate behavior that were positioned further away from us or who were not participating in our research. When participants and offenders who were close to us engaged in inappropriate behavior, and when we felt the behavior could not be ignored, we requested the behavior stop in a quick, professional, and courteous way. Once during data collection we asked an offender sitting in the front row who was masturbating to please put both hands on the table, and he complied. On another occasion, we asked two talkative offenders to please take the survey on their own without talking to their neighbor. When they refused to stop talking, we asked them to please bring their surveys to us, and we excused them from the data collection session. Overall, these were rare occasions, and we found that the vast majority of offenders treated us with the same courtesy, kindness, and respect that we showed them. Certainly, group data collection, like our jail study used, presents some challenges, as do all forms of data collection. However, this also had the benefit of obtaining a large number of surveys in a shorter period of time than one-on-one surveys do. There may be times, however, when it is necessary in institutions to terminate the interview or survey with a particular respondent, or even address an issue with a participant by talking to correctional staff. We suggest, however, that this strategy should be used only when necessary, to ensure trust is not broken between researchers and the people they are trying to study.

EDUCATION LEVEL AND LITERACY OF PEOPLE UNDER CORRECTIONAL CONTROL

Illiteracy is a serious problem among correctional populations (Coley and Barton 2006), although the published data on the educational levels of correctional populations are generally dated. About 40 percent of state prison inmates and 31 percent of probationers had not earned a high school degree or general equivalency diploma (Harlow 2003). The percentage of jail inmates without a degree was even higher (46.5%). Federal prison inmates tended to be more educated, with only about 27 percent having less than a high school education. This report found that men, minorities, younger inmates, and those raised without two parents were less likely to have a high school degree than were women, whites, older inmates, and those coming from two-parent families (Harlow 2003). The National Assessment of

Adult Literacy included inmates in their study population in 2003, finding that both women and men inmates had generally lower literacy than adults in the general population. They also found that those with less education had lower literacy (Greenberg et al. 2007).

Incarcerated juveniles are often at least one year, and often many years, behind their peers in grade level. Many "[i]ncarcerated youth have demonstrated significant reading, math, written and oral language deficits when compared to their nondelinquent peers" (Foley 2001, 253). In a more recent Arizona study, the authors reported that 30 percent of the population studied could be considered special education, while on average incarcerated youths were functioning below others on all measures they used to determine achievement. Results were worse for minority youths (Baltodano, Harris, and Rutherford 2005). In sum, academic achievement and literacy is generally a struggle for offenders in the correctional system. Findings show that educational achievement increases success upon release (see Davis et al. 2013, 2014). Consequently, there are often at least some efforts to put in place educational programs in adult incarceration facilities, and all juvenile incarceration facilities include educational components because laws require that youths have access to education (Davis et al. 2014).

ACCOMMODATING OFFENDERS' EDUCATION LEVELS

Given the differing levels of literacy and education among offenders, we recommend making survey and interview questions as straightforward and easy to interpret as possible. In other words, researchers should consider using simple rather than

PEACH CARD

Very Fair	**Somewhat Fair**	**Somewhat Unfair**	**Very Unfair**

ORANGE CARD

NONE	SOME	HALF	MOST	ALL

Figure 4. Example of an interview card to be handed to respondent. Source: Authors

complicated words regardless of the age of the target population. In most of our projects where we use interviews, we created interview cards with answer options on them to hand to participants as they answer questions. These cards are typically color coded (on colored card stock), half of an 8 ½ × 11 sheet, and laminated. We have multiple cards, each corresponding to a different answer set. See figure 4 for example answer cards used in the Florida Faith and Community-Based Delinquency Treatment Initiative evaluation. For example, we gave the orange card to youths while we asked about how many of their friends engaged in a list of activities (e.g., how many "had regularly taken part in church or religious activities," "had religious beliefs different from your own," "been suspended from school," "been in juvenile detention"). Codes for each question were on the interviewer's instrument. We have also seen (but not personally conducted) research with younger youths that use pictures such as smiley and sad faces to help them respond to interview questions.

When we administered surveys to jail inmates, we read all questions and response options aloud so that the participants who struggled with reading could follow along with us; however, participants were instructed to complete the survey at their own pace (e.g., 95% completed the survey at a faster pace). Additionally, a few participants requested one-on-one assistance completing the survey due to an inability to read. In these situations, one of us administered the survey to the larger group of participants while a research assistant helped individual participants.

When creating questions, it is important to remember how far removed the outside world is for some participants (e.g., while the average length of stay is twenty-three days for jail inmates, some prison inmates may have been incarcerated for decades). Therefore, questions about one's neighborhood, life on the streets, or life outside of the institution may elicit more recent memories for jail inmates or juveniles who often spend less time locked up in comparison to many prison inmates who have been incarcerated for a longer period of time. Of course, these sorts of questions will not be as current for them as would be for other correctional clients being managed in the community (i.e., those on probation and parole/conditional release). Consequently, if relevant, one should consider putting a time frame as part of the questions about life outside the walls. For example, one might ask about the neighborhood "in the year (month/week) before you came to this jail" or about what one anticipates happening upon release (right after release, within a few months or a year, etc.).

RESEARCH WITH NON-ENGLISH-SPEAKING PARTICIPANTS

Depending upon the research project and target population, it may be necessary or useful to offer the survey/interview questions in a language other than, or in addition to, English. As required by the IRB, it is important to anticipate ahead of time the language preferences of the people you will be researching, so you can have time to translate the instruments into another language(s) (see box 10). We have had success asking bilingual students to translate our instruments, and then had others translate the instruments back into English to make sure that the intended messages were conveyed in the translated version. It may also be possible to ask people in language departments at universities to translate instruments, sometimes for a fee. This translation may be all that is necessary if the surveys are self-administered (e.g., completed by the participant with pen/pencil). Yet, if questions will be asked by interviewers or survey questions may be read to people (e.g., in case of illiteracy concerns among participants), then it will be important to also have bilingual research assistants to conduct the interviews or read survey questions if the project leader cannot do so personally. Some universities have different IRB translation policies, depending upon whether the project is expedited or requires full board review (e.g., expedited projects may contain informal translation whereas full board approval projects sometimes require professional translators).

In our Florida jail project, we found that many bilingual inmates preferred to complete the Spanish version of the survey, even though they also spoke and read English fluently (e.g., Fox, Lane, and Zambrana 2011). We also observed that many of the Spanish-speaking inmates felt more comfortable sitting in a group of other Hispanic participants during data collection, which may reflect the tendency of inmates to sit with their own racial and ethnic groups anyway (e.g., see Irwin 2005; Ross and Richards 2002). While we do not know whether these participants would have completed the English version if a Spanish

BOX 10. BACK TRANSLATION AND CORRECTIONAL SETTINGS

"Back translation" is a process researchers use to ensure the correct translation of survey/interview questions across languages. Typically, one researcher creates the questions in English, another person translates the questions into the second language, and a third person translates the survey in the second language back to English. This allows the researcher to examine both English versions for consistency. Knowing about the dynamics and complexities of the second language is important for researchers to understand so that they may control key decisions about the translation. For example, the Spanish language uses both informal and formal terms for the exact same English words. To illustrate this point, the English word *you* is both *tú* (informal) or *usted* (formal) in Spanish, depending upon the familiarity of the other person. While we prefer to use more informal language (given literacy concerns with some offenders), we recommend consulting with a bilingual professional regarding the appropriateness of the formality for the target population. If research instruments are to be translated into another language, we strongly recommend spending time, effort, and money to execute the translation properly. Knowing whether your IRB has specific requirements about translations will be important (e.g., expedited reviews may not need a certified translator while full review protocols do). The World Health Organization (2016) offers more detailed advice for those interested in back translation.

version were unavailable, we believe having a Spanish version encouraged and increased participation among our relatively large population of Spanish-speaking offenders. Additionally, some IRBs may require instruments be offered in appropriate languages. As we have noted before, we believe it is important to do as much as possible to increase the comfort of participants, since it increases trust and openness.

Logistics of Collecting Data from Non-English-Speaking Participants

- During group announcements, first speak in English and then in other relevant language(s).

- If you do not speak the other language(s), consider finding research assistants who do. This is critical if researchers will be personally administering the instruments (i.e., reading them) rather than letting the respondents complete them on their own.

- If in an institution, depending upon the administration procedures, it may be efficient to administer the questions in both English and other language(s) simultaneously in separate areas of the correctional facility.

- If data collection will occur with respondents individually (e.g., in interviews), researchers should ensure that bilingual research assistants are matched with respondents who are bilingual or monolingual in other languages.

- Bilingual researchers should carry the instruments in the relevant languages to allow them to administer the participant's preferred version on-the-spot.

- When preparing for data entry, ensure coding to identify the language the survey/interview was administered to facilitate checks for any differences in the analyses.

CORRECTIONAL POPULATIONS WITH SPECIAL NEEDS

Of the correctional population, participants with special needs may very well represent the majority—not the minority. Special needs affect many more people than those with psychological or physical disabilities. Correctional populations with special needs may also include people who are racial/ethnic minorities; indigenous; lesbian, gay, bisexual, or transgender (LGBT); older/elderly; younger/juvenile; terminally ill; and those serving a death sentence (United Nations Office on Drugs and Crime 2009). Additionally, pregnant women, parents (especially single parents of dependent children), and other primary caregivers have special needs.

Those with special needs may be particularly vulnerable, above and beyond the vulnerability experienced by other correctional populations, and they need additional consideration and protection. Identifying and addressing participants' special needs can be very challenging for researchers. Safeguards or accommodations for participants with special needs will depend on the type of research and the nature of what participants are asked to do. Because the term *special needs* can mean many things, it is impossible for us to offer the same degree of practical advice here as we do on other topics throughout this book. By carefully considering whether there are reasonable safeguards for those in the target population with special needs, researchers can often enhance the research experience and improve the quality of the results. This may be as simple as including additional questions or response options that take into consideration the status/lifestyle of those with special needs. Other helpful accommodations may include changing the method of recruiting participants, altering where participants are located during the research, adjusting data collection instruments, reading aloud to illiterate participants, or showing pictures of emotions to children who may be too young to articulate their feelings. It is wise for researchers to talk with correctional staff during project conceptualization to identify special needs and safeguards that may affect the research project.

PILOTING THE DATA COLLECTION INSTRUMENTS

Piloting data collection instruments before administering to the target population (so improvements can be made) is very beneficial; yet, it can be challenging to find a sample of people similar to the target population. If the target population is correctional officers or staff members, then similar groups of professionals that may be accessible for piloting instruments may be police cadets, halfway house staff, or drug/alcohol treatment staff. If the target population is offenders, then accessible offenders in the community for piloting instruments may be parolees, clients of specialty courts (e.g., drug court offenders, domestic violence court offenders, veterans' court offenders), clients of drug/alcohol treatment centers, or clients of local offender programs, including shelters. Of course, if one is planning to sample from a particular community population, it is important to be careful not to include them in the pilot study unless they would not be included in the study population anyway (e.g., they would complete probation or be released from incarceration before the actual study started or are in a dormitory or institution that would not be included anyway). Otherwise, including them in the pilot prohibits their inclusion in the final sample and may reduce the final sample size. In other words, the pilot data should not be included in the study's analysis.

We have had success piloting a survey instrument with undergraduate students and clients of a local drug court (Fox, Lane, and Zambrana 2011). The students were offered extra credit for participating, and the drug court clients were offered community service credit hours. Other times, we have piloted instruments with people already being served before the actual study was implemented. Based on the tremendously helpful feedback from the pilot groups, we implemented important changes prior to finalizing instrument. For example, regarding a survey question asking whether respondents had ever been shot, one pilot participant suggested that we add important clarification that the incident was not military related. Another pilot participant made very skilled edits to Grasmick and colleagues' (1993) self-control scale to streamline the wording (e.g., original question: "I don't devote much thought or effort to preparing for the future" was shortened to "I don't think much about the future."). In our South Oxnard Challenge Project (SOCP) evaluation, we used a validated scale in the youth interview, which used the word "brood," meaning worry, and we realized that many youths did not understand the word. Although we kept the word in the final instrument, we gave our research assistants guidance on how to respond if youths did not understand the meaning of the word. Changing the question wording may present some methodological issues in terms of validity, reliability, or for comparison purposes that researchers may wish to avoid, so these decisions need to be made carefully. In sum, we highly recommend piloting instruments on a group similar to the target population.

TIME-CONSUMING SETBACKS AND THE IMPORTANCE OF RESEARCHER FLEXIBILITY

Over the years and on many projects, we have encountered numerous time-consuming setbacks even before setting foot inside adult and juvenile correctional facilities or starting projects in probation or parole settings. Gaining approval to access correctional populations can be a time-consuming endeavor, a topic that is discussed in detail within this book. In this section we highlight examples of instances where delays often occur after access has been granted and before/during data collection efforts.

We recommend confirming appointments, no matter whom the researcher is planning to meet. It is useful to do this the day before, and sometimes again the day of the meeting. Multiple personal phone contacts are often preferable if meeting correctional clients in the community, for example. Offenders often have difficult, unstable lives (Petersilia 2003) and so they may or may not show for appointments. If they do not show up, it may or may not mean they do not want to participate. They might just be forgetful, not keep a calendar, lack transportation, or be struggling with something else more important. Consequently, it is useful in project planning to make a decision about the number of follow-up contacts project researchers will make with correctional clients before giving up on particular participants.

It also is not unusual for correctional staff inside and outside facilities to have issues pop up that require rescheduling appointments with researchers. For example, some agencies rescheduled data collection with us in the past due to time conflicts that arose for the staff members who would be our escorts while in the facility. Others have forgotten appointments completely and had to reschedule due to double booking. Sometimes unexpected emergencies arise. We once waited hours at a correctional facility only to finally learn that our agency contact was home sick. After additional time-consuming delays, another staff member eventually was assigned to escort us throughout the facility. At another facility we waited nearly three hours for correctional staff to finish watching television before escorting us to the dormitories after issuing our identification badges at the administration building (despite our frequent and polite requests to proceed). Of course, we do not know if there were other things going in the facility that prevented our entry that could not be shared with us. Although in our jail study, we never had to reschedule for a different day completely once we arrived at the facilities, we did encounter setbacks that delayed data collection and resulted in time-consuming administrative tasks. In other studies, we have had times when unexpected events arose at an institution, and we needed to leave and come back another day to conduct the research with staff. If unexpected events arise and meetings need to be rescheduled, researchers may deal with other inconveniences such as rescheduling with research assistants, rental car, and hotel reservations if traveling to another area to collect data.

Once data collection began, we also often experienced setbacks. At times, respondents, especially people in the community, came to the interview under the influence of drugs or clearly appeared to be lying to us, not taking the research seriously, and so on. Consequently, most of our instruments, especially interview instruments, contain a final page for the interviewer to complete to assess the situation. See figure 5 for an example interviewer assessment form we have used. This page often includes questions allowing the interviewer to rate the reliability of the answers given, the

---

[INTERVIEWER: COMPLETE THIS SECTION AFTER THE YOUTH HAS LEFT THE SITE]

1. How would you rate the answers given to you?

Very reliable......................................	1
Reliable..	2
Marginally reliable.........................	3
Unreliable......................................	4
Very unreliable..............................	5

2. Overall, how attentive was youth during the Interview?

Attentive.......................................	1
Somewhat inattentive or uninvolved...	2
Easily distracted, needed urging to pay attention, or often required repetition of questions..................	3

3. Did youth get less attentive as the Interview proceeded?

Not at all	1
A little less......................................	2
A lot less	3

COMMENTS:

_____

_____

_____

_____

_____

_____

Figure 5. Interviewer assessment form. Source: Authors

attentiveness of the respondent, whether the respondent's focus changed as the interview progressed, and whether the participant seemed to understand the questions. There is also an open-ended section for the interviewer to comment if relevant.

A few times, in institutions, plans to enter a specific dormitory to collect data were derailed for a number of reasons, including unscheduled lockdowns, meetings (e.g., religious services, group therapy), and commissary distribution. Lockdowns occur when prison or jail staff detain inmates in their cells by locking a housing unit for any number of reasons. These are very common and they prevent anyone—including researchers—from moving to or from particular places (such as dorms or units) within correctional facilities. This can mean delays that can last minutes or hours. On numerous occasions, the person who approved our research did not notify correctional staff about our study prior to our arrival. This necessitated that we, or our escort, spend time reintroducing ourselves and explaining the purpose of our visit to every supervisor in every dormitory we entered. Researchers may find it useful to carry the permission letter from the administrators; however, a repeated verbal explanation of the researcher's identity and purpose is often needed. In some instances, it was necessary to relocate participants to multipurpose rooms because this offered a more quiet and private environment for data collection than the dormitory; however, we frequently had to wait for the rooms to become available as they were often used for religious services, educational classes, and meetings with attorneys. During one data collection session, an inmate experienced a seizure, and we were required to vacate the dormitory and wait until order had been regained before reentering. On another occasion, a fight among inmates prevented us from accessing the last dormitory on the last planned day of data collection, which necessitated another six-hour drive for a return trip to the facility for a forty-five-minute data collection session.

These examples underscore the importance of researcher patience and flexibility. Collecting data in correctional settings means that researchers must quickly adapt to the rules and events (planned and spontaneous). And despite good intentions and best efforts, some setbacks are an inevitable part of the experience. These sorts of delays at the start can be very frustrating and discouraging, too, if they are not anticipated. It is important for researchers in this area to understand that these sorts of problems are more typical than not. It is all part of doing research, especially in the criminal justice system where unexpected events are typical.

Tips to Minimize Time-Consuming Delays Prior to
Data Collection

- Confirm the appointment, ideally by calling or e-mailing in the early morning to allow time for any needed follow-ups.

- If meeting someone in the community, agree to meet at a time and location that is most convenient for the respondent, even if it is not your preferred time or place (as long as it is safe).

- If going to an institution, request that appropriate staff be notified of the purpose and date of the visit (and offer, as a courtesy, to send a draft statement that can be easily modified).

- If correctional facilities or staff will be gatekeepers, bring a permission letter from headquarters or administration to all meetings.

- Request a list of any scheduled activities at institutions or probation or parole offices that may delay data collection, and avoid scheduling meetings or data collection during those periods. Consider discussing with administrators an alternative plan for collecting data in the event that a scheduled or unscheduled event occurs.

- Arrive early at appointments in case there are issues that need to be resolved before data collection can start.

- Create a list of all materials needed for data collection (personal identification, pens/pencils, forms, tape recorders [if allowed], payments for incentives, receipts for incentives, etc.) and double-check that all are in the research bag or box before leaving for the appointment. Also ensure that these materials are collected before exiting the research location.

IMPORTANCE OF RECORD KEEPING

We cannot overemphasize the importance of maintaining organized records during all phases of data collection. You may wish to keep several different "trackers" or logs, depending upon personal preferences and the dynamics involved with each unique project. The following are some examples of the trackers we maintained electronically (and backed up in multiple places).

Access Tracker

One of our access trackers documented all communication with correctional agencies in our attempt to gain access to conduct the research. Each entry in this spreadsheet was organized by date of communication, and contained the following information for each person we talked with: phone number, e-mail address (if applicable), full name, title/position, date of contact, whether a voice message was left, and status of the communication (e.g., waiting to hear about approval, missed return call/need to call again). We also have created contact logs for potential interview respondents, whether they be correctional staff or clients. These also typically contain contact information (address, phone number, e-mail address), why they are contacted (e.g., staff or type of client), dates of contact, status of communication (e.g., interview or meeting date, time, and place or time/date to follow up or refusal and reason if available). Because some people may need to be contacted multiple times before data collection or need to be contacted for follow-ups, it is often important to have one contact sheet for each person, maybe in a transportable binder, as well as a summary file in Excel. In addition, when researchers anticipate the need to contact the person for a scheduled follow-up (e.g., at six, twelve, or eighteen months post–random assignment or first contact), it is important to also gather information at the initial interview about how to contact the person at a later date, including addresses, phone numbers, e-mail addresses, and contact information for people who would know how to reach them (see Hall and colleagues' (2003) tracking document available online).

Data Tracker

One of our data trackers used in institutions for group survey administration documented all data collection sessions, including: date, facility, pod/dormitory, time data collection began (in each pod/meaning each session), time data collection ended (in each pod/meaning each session), total time in data collection (time ended minus time began), number of participants, population size, gender of unit/participants, researcher who conducted survey/interview administration, number of participants in Spanish versus English survey/interview administration, and any problems that arose. Others contained a list of those interviewed, including similar information, such as name, date of interview, length of interview, the time the interview started and stopped, the location of the interview, and so forth. Given that the access and data trackers often contain identifiable information, they will most likely need to be kept in a secure location depending upon IRB requirements.

Decision Logs

Another critically important task is to maintain a project decision log. This can be a journal or a word processing document, but it should include each decision made, the date made, and the reasoning behind the decision. One should record all decisions that affect the project. Examples of decisions to log include: whom to sample, how many, what types of data to collect, what questions to include in the instruments, how often to collect data from participants, and why data collection efforts changed (e.g., instruments were modified midproject, no more people were interviewed, or follow-ups were not completed). This information is very important, because project reports often occur months or years after data collection decisions were made, and it is difficult to remember the reasoning behind each decision unless it is recorded. Journal reviewers also often ask about why choices were made, and this log makes responding to those sorts of comments much easier.

TRAVELING TO CORRECTIONAL
FACILITIES AND POPULATIONS

Correctional facilities are typically in locations that are relatively removed from places most people frequent. They tend to be in the outskirts where land is less expensive and less visible.

This means the mere act of getting to the front doors of correctional facilities is usually very time consuming and often requires a substantial amount of driving time through sometimes very rural areas. We have traveled great distances on numerous occasions to correctional facilities (sometimes driving six or more hours one way). In addition to the immense time required to get to and from correctional facilities, there are many other costs when planning this type of travel. Sometimes grant funds can be used to fund data collection trips. However, on projects with little or no funding, the costs may come out of pocket. For example, on our jail project we accumulated a few thousand dollars in rental car, gas, and hotel costs (not to mention food), of which the majority was paid personally after university and grant funding ran out. However, rental car companies and hotels do often offer discounted rates for state employees, which can reduce costs somewhat. These costs are one of the reasons that people might consider seeking grant funding to do correctional research.

Preparations before and after travel to correctional facilities are also time consuming. Our checklists before traveling often included: pick up rental car, fill car with gas, put envelope in glove box to keep all receipts, refill box of research materials (e.g., informed consents in English and Spanish, surveys in English and Spanish, pencils), prepare "prison clothes" for the morning, confirm pick up with research assistant(s), confirm data collection appointment with correctional contact, and stock car with water bottles, mints/lozenges, files containing contact information, directions to the facility, and any precautions or instructions from correctional facility. We have often found that GPS mapping does not work well when accessing institutions in remote and rural areas, so we recommend obtaining specific driving instructions (including maps) directly from the institution's website and/or your agency contact. After data collection we transferred notes to electronic files regarding data collection procedures (see "Importance of Record Keeping" above), numbered completed surveys, sent thank you messages to correctional contacts, returned the rental car (with a full tank of gas), reconciled receipts and expenses, and locked completed and numbered surveys in a filing cabinet on campus to be entered electronically later by research assistants.

Although it may sound like we brought a lot of materials into correctional facilities (e.g., boxes of surveys, informed consents, pencils), we were only permitted to bring the bare minimum, especially in terms of personal items. Some facilities will not allow pens and pencils from the outside, for example, because they can be stolen and used as weapons. Facilities often have special writing implements that are flexible and made especially for correctional institutions, which you may be required to use.

Before traveling to the correctional facility, we strongly recommend asking for a list of exact items (personal and research materials) that will be allowed inside. Mistakes or oversights on your part will likely result in time-consuming delays (e.g., waiting for administrative personnel to confirm that particular item is not permitted inside and a trip back out to your vehicle to secure unapproved materials). Leave cell phones in your vehicle out of sight. The only unapproved items we brought in to correctional facilities were our car keys, which were left with the reception staff or secured in a very small locked cubbyhole/locker. The adage "less is more" is key when it comes to bringing things into correctional facilities.

These sorts of procedures also occur when we interview people outside of correctional facilities. Although there are typically much fewer restrictions on what researchers can bring to other data collection sites, it is important to ask about these rules if researchers are meeting clients at a probation or parole office, for example. Or, if meeting in a public place, it is important to consider what to bring both for research and safety purposes (e.g., pens, pencils, consent forms, paper instruments, multiple tape or voice recorders in case one stops working, extra batteries, summaries of the project or flyers, cell phones, laptops, etc.).

WHERE TO CONDUCT THE RESEARCH

Research Inside Correctional Facilities

Understanding the general layout of the jail, prison, or juvenile detention center can help researchers work with staff to find a safe and relatively quiet place to conduct the research. Protecting participants' privacy and ensuring everyone's safety is of utmost importance. For example, is there a semiprivate room within the dayroom in the jail or prison that can easily be used for data collection? Or will inmates participate at the tables in the dayroom while nonparticipants are moved to their rooms (or vice versa)? Alternatively, will participants be removed to a separate location for data collection (e.g., multipurpose room, chapel, or classroom)? We have collected data in all of these types of locations and more (including a storage closet with windows). Allowing the facility to determine where data collection occurs is one way of being as unobtrusive as possible while inside the walls. While moving participants to a private or semiprivate location is more time consuming, these settings are ideal because they offer the most privacy for participants. However, relocating participants is not always possible or realistic. When participants are seated in the tables in the open dayroom, nonparticipants can (and do) sometimes approach this area out of curiosity in the project. To protect participants' privacy, it is critical to politely ask nonparticipants to give participants privacy by moving away from the area. In some situations, such as when a pencil and paper survey is being administered to a group of inmates at one time, it also may be appropriate to walk the perimeter of the data collection area separating participants and nonparticipants while asking nonparticipants to distance themselves from participants. We realize some researchers may not be comfortable positioning themselves so close to inmates while giving instructions for nonparticipants to move, even though a correctional officer may be in the room supervising.

An alternative approach may be to request that correctional officers help ensure that nonparticipants maintain an appropriate distance from participants. However, in our Florida jail study, we avoided this approach whenever possible for a couple of reasons. Specifically, we wished to control the situation ourselves when possible, rather than rely on correctional officers who might give commands in an authoritarian—instead of assertive—way. In other words, we felt as if we maintained rapport with participants by avoiding an overreliance on officers. Additionally, we wanted to avoid creating any more work for correctional officers, who were responsible for supervising the entire population in the dorm and not just the group of inmates affecting us.

If officer observation is necessary for safety, it would be ideal to meet in a room with glass for viewing but not within earshot of staff or other correctional clients. In this case, we would recommend having the participant's back to the window, so no one could read lips to discern answers. A similar approach could be used if conducting a focus group. If data collection is occurring in a group (e.g., survey administration), it would be useful to ask participants to cover their papers as they answer. While one presumably would not be unsafe with correctional officers while conducting interviews, similar procedures might be useful when they are the participants. That is, private rooms not within earshot of others and not where someone can see enough to try to guess what they are saying are ideal. If completing surveys independently, officers and staff could be allowed to submit their responses through the mail and be given a self-addressed, stamped envelope or to submit their surveys in a locked drop box at the facility or agency office to which only the research team has access.

Research Outside Correctional Facilities

If interviews are occurring with staff or clients outside of institutions, similar concerns are relevant. First, interviews should occur in places that are safe and but private, or at least out of earshot of others. For example, we have often conducted interviews in back corners of restaurants or in a public park. For privacy at a restaurant, a table should be sought in the back of those settings, with the participant facing and projecting his/her voice to the researcher, who is seated along a back wall. In our SOCP study, we had researchers on location in their own office and often conducted interviews with staff and youths in that office with the door shut, although we also went to public places and staff offices when that was most convenient for the participant. In public places, there is no safety protection from correctional staff generally, so it is important for researchers to consider safety concerns and their own comfort level. It is also necessary to consider the safety and comfort level of research assistants, which may be different than one's own level of ease. Some researchers might want to notify others involved in the research project of their interview time and location with other people involved in the research project as a safety precaution.

OTHER THINGS TO CONSIDER

What Should a Researcher Do When They Have to Use the Bathroom Inside a Correctional Facility?

Correctional staff will likely escort or direct researchers to the restroom, although this may take some time to move in and out of secured areas. To secure research materials, consider either leaving the materials with a member of the research team (not the correctional staff) or bringing the materials into the restroom if conducting the data collection alone.

What Can Researchers Do to Minimize the Risk of Contracting Communicable Diseases from Correctional Populations?

Because of offenders' close proximity to each other, coupled with reduced access to preventative health care, correctional institutions can be breeding grounds for some diseases. To minimize researchers' risk of contracting communicable diseases, follow the general recommendations that are routinely publicized by the Centers for Disease Control and Prevention (e.g., regularly wash hands, stay updated with vaccinations). We have also excluded from our research the inmates housed in communicable disease units. Keeping hand sanitizer in researchers' vehicles may also help minimize exposure to diseases.

How Do Researchers Make Small Talk with Offenders
Who Are Convicted of Serious Crimes (e.g., Someone
Serving Six Consecutive Life Sentences with
No Chance of Parole)?

In addition to talking about sports, which we mentioned earlier as our preferred way to build rapport with offenders, researchers might also discuss other general topics that offenders know about such as the weather, TV shows, hobbies, or books the offenders are reading.

Should Researchers Report Unprofessional Behavior by a
Correctional Officer or Medical Professional?

There is a wide range of unprofessional behavior that *could* occur, although we found this to be very rare. Some unprofessional behavior is relatively minor and might not be necessary to report. For example, during data collection in one facility a correctional officer briefly shined a flashlight in the faces of some participants to distract them. While we found this behavior to be unprofessional and disruptive, it was brief and at the end of our data collection efforts, so we elected not to report the behavior to our administrative contact. Other forms of unprofessional behavior must be reported to administrative contacts and/or the IRB, although we have never personally experienced this. Research assistants should report all unprofessional behavior to the lead researcher so the lead researcher can decide who must be notified. The correctional facility may also provide a list of rules before entering the facility, which might include whom to contact if there is a problem.

How Do Researchers Cope with Stress or Feelings After
Leaving the Correctional Facility at the End of the Day?

This can be particularly challenging, even for seasoned scholars. Because correctional facilities are often located in remote locations that require far drives from campus or home, this often leaves a lot of time for researchers and research assistants to process the day's data collection efforts. In our experience, we often found these long drives to be productive times to think quietly and talk through our experiences with the other research team members. When riding in teams or pairs, we often also used this time to record relevant project data, especially on the happenings of the day, the context of the data collection, or the perceptions of situations that occurred. We often find it useful to have the passenger type on a laptop or tablet while the debriefing occurs, so immediate thoughts are not lost as the research progresses over time. If someone happens to experience a high level of stress, it is important that they communicate this to the lead researcher with whom matters can be discussed and potentially make arrangements for assistance from a university or independent counselor.

How Do Researchers Prevent Participants from
Becoming Distressed Due to the Nature of the Study?

Although researchers implement many safeguards prior to data collection to reduce the likelihood that participants may become distressed (e.g., the informed consent process and trust building), it is important to provide participants with a realistic resource (or two) that they may seek out if needed. If participants are inmates, then a prison/jail psychologist or counselor might be a viable option. If participants are not incarcerated (e.g., parolees, probationers, or staff members), then community resources may be helpful. In any case, seeking help should be free of charge for participants and requests for permission to list agencies or individuals on informed consent documents should be made in the early stages of the project, prior to data collection. In some cases, IRBs may require contacts for publicly available resources be listed on consent forms.

CONCLUSION

There are so many aspects involved with conducting research with correctional populations that can easily overwhelm many researchers—even seasoned scholars. It is our hope that the information in this book and our experiences will help those encountering correctional populations feel and be more prepared and more confident. Of course, interacting with people in general—and correctional populations in particular—always yields new and unexpected experiences. While this book contains our "insider's perspective" into the world of researching correctional populations, there are undoubtedly many other circumstances and situations that researchers can encounter. We could not possibly discuss everything we have learned over the years. Yet, the possibility of new experiences is part of what makes research with correctional populations so unique and interesting. Regardless of the method one uses to study correctional populations, we wish to emphasize the importance of being prepared, organized, patient, and professional. Navigating the necessary nitty-gritty details associated with researching correctional populations can be challenging, time consuming, and expensive, but it is also exciting, important, and professionally rewarding.

AGENCY LETTER OF SUPPORT

Date

[Insert researcher name and address]

Dear [insert researcher name],

I am writing to express strong support for your U.S. Department of Justice grant proposal under the following program [insert grant solicitation name here]. We would be pleased to cooperate with you and your team.

Your grant proposal includes conducting strategic planning to enhance the services we offer our clients. Our clients include violent offenders of interpersonal crimes, including sexual violence, domestic abuse, and stalking.

Strategic planning is essential for our organization. Your research will allow us to better understand how efficiently and effectively our organization operates to help sexual and domestic violence offenders become rehabilitated and reintegrated into their communities. Your strategic plan will also give us important insight about any unmet client needs that we may improve upon in the future to increase the effectiveness of our services.

We agree to fully cooperate with you and your team as you conduct the strategic planning. Our agency will allow you to access client records, interview personnel and clients, and collect other agency information that you may need, including financial records.

I have read and support your grant proposal. Our organization is excited about collaborating with you. We look forward to partnering with you. This strategic planning will be instrumental for helping our organization better serve the needs of the community by helping to rehabilitate violent offenders.

Sincerely,

Executive Director

WEEKLY CONTACT SHEET FOR STAFF WITH CLIENT CASELOADS IN THE EXPERIMENTAL (SOCP) GROUP

South Oxnard Challenge Project
Weekly Contact Report

Client Name _____

CSA # _____

Recorder _____

Week Begins (Sunday) _____

Year _____

PLEASE NOTE: Forms are due Monday of the following week.

RECORDER POSITION

1. DPO
2. Navigator
3. Alcohol & Drug
4. Mental Health
5. Recreation
6. Protective Services
7. Community Outreach Worker
8. Police

(Circle One)
9. Navigator Supervisor
10. Senior DPO
11. Service Coordinator
12. City Corps
13. Mediator
14. PDAP
15. Team Leader (Other than Senior DPO)

(1) DATE OF CONTACT mo/day/yr	(2) TARGET OF CONTACT see codes below	(3) TYPE OF CONTACT see codes below	(4) CONTACT PURPOSE see codes below	(5) TEAM MEMBERS PRESENT (INVOLVED) see codes below	(6) TIME LENGTH OF CONTACT in minutes	(7) PO ONLY YOUTH TECHNICAL VIOLATIONS see codes below					(8) PO ONLY # YOUTH (FRESH) ARRESTS			(9) Restitution Paid (in $)	(10) Community Service Hours Completed (if other than City Corps) (number of hours)	(11) ADDITIONAL COMMENTS
						Code	If filed, indicate charge	Date filed	Init. Dept (see codes)		Charge(s) by PC/WI/BP code	Date			

(1) DATE OF CONTACT
mo/day/yr

(2) TARGET(s)
y - youth   f - family
v - victim   vf - victim's family

(3) TYPE OF CONTACT
PC - phone contact   LC - letter contact
OV - office visit   RV - residence visit
WV - workplace visit   SV - school visit
OV - institutional visit CV - community visit
CC - collateral contact AC - attempted contact
OTH - other, please specify

(4) CONTACT PURPOSE
SEE ATTACHED CODE SHEET (iclude all that apply)

(5) TEAM MEMBERS PRESENT
PO - probation officer   PS - probation supervisor
SDPO - senior DPO   SC - service coordinator
N - navigator   NS - navigator supervisor
AD - alcohol & drug specialist MD - mediator
MH - mental health specialist CPS - protective services specialist
PLC - police officer   COW - community outreach worker
REC - recreation worker   CC - City Corps
PDAP - PDAP counselor   TL - team leader

(6) TIME LENGTH OF CONTACT
in minutes

(7) TECHNICAL VIOL. CODES
(include all that apply on separate lines)
F - fines   TV - treatment violation
R - failure to report   AB - abscond
RES - restitution   C - curfew
A - alcohol related D - drug related
S - school   ST - status related
OTH - other, specify

(8) FRESH ARRESTS
a. Initiating department   OXPD - Oxnard Police
   SD - sheriff's department   OTH - please specify
   PHD - Port Hueneme Police   c. Indicate date of arrest
b. Indicate charge

(9) RESTITUTION Indicate amount of restitution paid

(10) COMMUNITY SERVICE HOURS Indicate number of hours other than City Corps

(11) ADDITIONAL COMMENTS indicate any relevant additional information

YOUR ASSESSMENT OF THIS WEEK'S CHALLENGE PLAN PROGRESS
(Circle Appropriate Number)

AREA	Very Poor	Poor	Adequate	Good	Very Good	Unable to Evaluate	Comments/Planned Response
Individual	1	2	3	4	5	8	
Family	1	2	3	4	5	8	
School	1	2	3	4	5	8	
Peers	1	2	3	4	5	8	
Community	1	2	3	4	5	8	

(form rev 7/28/98)

WEEKLY CONTACT CODE SHEET FOR STAFF WITH CLIENT CASELOADS IN THE EXPERIMENTAL (SOCP) GROUP

ARR	arrange meeting/appt./FC
FC	family conference to talk about CP or sign agreements
PS	problem solving with youth or family or both
PT	check status of probation terms
SRCH	probation search
SPA	sign probation agreement
SCA	sign challenge agreement
CA	check compliance with challenge agreement
UA	urinalysis test (indicate if dirty)
BT	breath test (indicate if dirty)
ICS	individual (therapeutic) counseling session
GCS	group (therapeutic) counseling session
MN	mentoring
TU	tutoring
FEM	facilitate employment
FED	facilitate education
FS	facilitate services/ referral to services
SKL	administer skills test

CMON	monitor community service
RMON	monitor/check participation tutoring, recreation activities, etc.
TRANS	transport to Challenge or other services
TREC	transport to and/ or participate in recreation activities
MSA	monitor school attendance, behavior, grades
MED	mediation (indicate with whom)
CI	crisis intervention (e.g., addressing an immediate crisis)
CM	crisis management (e.g., dealing with family arguments)
INT	interview
NA	needs assessment
SI	share information with other agency
CC	case conference
NOT	family or youth contacts you to notify you of something (e.g., missing school or activity)
TLK	just to talk
RST	determine restitution
COMC	community contact related to youth
INTR	introduce yourself/project
TRM	terminate contract (end program participation)
OTH	other (please specify)

MST ONLY

MHI	Mental Health Intake
FCS	Family Counseling Session

RECREATION STAFF ONLY

RSVY	recreation survey
RPLN	create recreation plan
RPMN	monitoring individual rec. plan

PUBLICALLY AVAILABLE DATA SOURCES

Federal Bureau of Investigation. Uniform Crime Report. https://ucr
.fbi.gov/

Inter-university Consortium for Political and Social Research
(ICPSR). https://www.icpsr.umich.edu/icpsrweb/

U.S. Department of Justice. Bureau of Justice Statistics. National
Crime Victimization Survey. http://www.bjs.gov/index.cfm?ty=
dcdetail&iid=245

U.S. Department of Justice. Bureau of Justice Statistics. National Prisoner Statistics (NPS)

U.S. Department of Justice. Bureau of Justice Statistics. Survey of
Inmates in Federal Corrections Facilities (SIFCF)

U.S. Department of Justice. Bureau of Justice Statistics. Survey of
Inmates in State Correctional Facilities (SISCF)

"THINKING FOR A CHANGE" FACILITATOR PEER RATING FORM

Florida Department of Juvenile Justice

If you have questions, contact Dr. Jodi Lane at the University of Florida. jlane@ufl.edu or [phone]

Facility:		
Date of Group:		
Start Time:	End Time:	
Facilitator 1: (Name)		Name of Person Completing This Form
Facilitator 2: (Name)		Title of Person Completing This Form
Lesson Number:	Group Size:	

Section 1: Mechanics of Lesson

Please indicate your opinion of how well the facilitator(s) did the following in today's lesson (circle number that corresponds to your rating):

	Not at all	Needs Some Improvement	Adequate	Very Well	Excellent
1. Cover the entire lesson	1	2	3	4	5
a. Review homework	1	2	3	4	5
b. Model new skill (staff)	1	2	3	4	5
c. Role play (youth)	1	2	3	4	5
d. Give feedback on role play	1	2	3	4	5
e. Explain new homework	1	2	3	4	5
f. Assign new homework	1	2	3	4	5
g. Cover all activities in manual	1	2	3	4	5
2. Meet stated objectives of lesson	1	2	3	4	5

Section 2: Experiential Component of Lesson

Please rate the facilitator's teaching today in terms of:

	Poor	Needs Some Improvement	Adequate	Good	Excellent
3. Preparation (materials ready, lesson well planned, knowledge of material)	1	2	3	4	5
4. Comfort level teaching lesson	1	2	3	4	5
5. Objectivity (presented factually, without moralizing or opinion/nonjudgmental)	1	2	3	4	5
6. Clarity (covering content clearly)	1	2	3	4	5
7. Simplicity (no unnecessary complication/using terms youth understand)	1	2	3	4	5
8. Pacing (not too rushed, not too slow)	1	2	3	4	5
9. Engagement (presented in interesting way, participants involved)	1	2	3	4	5

GENERAL INFORMED CONSENT FOR TRADITIONAL PLACEMENTS IN THE FLORIDA FAITH AND COMMUNITY-BASED DELINQUENCY TREATMENT INITIATIVE (FCBDTI)

JUVENILE'S NAME: _____

You will be considered for residential placement. Florida's Department of Juvenile Justice is working with an agency of the national Department of Justice in Washington, D.C. in developing new programs. The national agency wants to know how well programs work. Independent researchers from the University of Florida will be studying programs in Florida and will choose a sample from those of you who are eligible for residential placement in this area. Youth will be selected for the study by chance rather than because of who they are. Researchers may ask you to help with this research, but before you can help, you and your parent or guardian need to give consent. Participation in the research will be voluntary. You would be able to withdraw from the research at any time. There is no penalty for not participating.

Researchers from the University of Florida may want to talk with you, your parent or guardian, juvenile justice staff, and others to learn about your commitment program and its impact. The researchers will also look at your official records. Signing this form gives consent for this research to be done but does not require you or anyone to answer questions for the researchers. Nothing will happen to you if you refuse to participate in the research or answer their questions. You will not receive any benefits or compensation for your participation. The researchers may talk with you and give you some questions to answer. They may meet with you 2-4 times during your sentence, but no meeting with you will last longer than an hour. The researchers may also visit the program to see first-hand what happens. The information that the researchers get will not be shared in a way that identifies you. It will be locked in a file at the university and will be stored using a code number rather than your name. When the study is complete, the names of those who participated will be destroyed. In other words, the researchers will protect your confidentiality to the extent provided by law to minimize any risks that may otherwise result from participating.

The final decision for placement resides with the Commitment Manager of the Department of Juvenile Justice. Participation in the program research will not give you special privileges and it will not shorten your length of stay or reduce time in aftercare. Release from your residential placement and aftercare supervision depends on your successful completion of the program. As is true in all commitment programs, noncompliance with program rules and misbehavior could result in your transfer to another residential facility.

By signing this form, you and your parent or guardian give consent to be part of this research if you are chosen. If you have questions or concerns about the research, you may contact: Professor Lonn Lanza-Kaduce or Professor Jodi Lane [address and phone number). If you have questions about your rights as a

participant in this research, you may contact the UFIRB Office, [address and phone number].

_____   _____
Juvenile's Signature   **Parent/Guardian Signature**

EXAMPLE OF RE-CONSENT FOR YOUTHS PARTICIPATING IN THE FAITH AND COMMUNITY-BASED DELINQUENCY TREATMENT INITIATIVE (FCBDTI)

Protocol title:

Evaluation of Faith and Community Initiative (# 2004-U-581)
Reminder of research study: When you were sent here, you were told that this program was trying new things to help young people like you, and that research would be done to see how everything is working. You and your parent or guardian agreed that it would be all right for us to do this research. We want to learn about you and the program so we can find out how well it's working. So we are asking whether we can talk with you.

What you will be asked to do in the study:

You will be asked questions. Most of the questions will have a set of possible answers for you to choose from. The choices will be shown to you on cards so that you can pick the one that's best for you. For example, sometimes you will be asked if you strongly agree, agree, disagree, or strongly disagree with something. For some questions, you will not need a card and you can just answer it. For example, how old you are. The researcher will mark your answers on a form.

Time required:

The questions should take less than an hour.

Benefits:

You will not directly benefit from answering these questions. **YOU WILL NOT BE PAID OR RECEIVE ANYTHING. YOU WILL NOT BE TREATED DIFFERENTLY OR RELEASED EARLIER.** Our hope is that what we learn will help make programs for young people better in the future.

Risks and confidentiality:

Your answers pose little risk to you. Your identity will be kept confidential to the extent provided by law. That means we are not going to tell anyone that it was you who said something. There are two exceptions: we **must tell** others if you report to us that you <u>have been abused</u> and we **have to tell** others if you report to us that you <u>plan to hurt someone</u>. We will put a code number instead of your name on the form. The list that connects your name to the code will be kept in a locked file in the research office at the University of Florida. No one but the researchers will see your answers. When the study is complete, the list will be torn up. Your name will not be used in any report.

Voluntary participation:

You do not have to answer the questions. Your participation is completely voluntary. Nothing bad will happen to you if you do not help out.

Right to withdraw from the study:

You can stop answering questions at any time; nothing will happen to you as a result. You may choose to answer most questions but refuse to answer some of them. That's ok too. Just tell us to skip a question you do not want to answer.

Whom to contact if you have questions about the study:

If you have questions about the research, you may contact Professor Jodi Lane [address & phone number]

Whom to contact about your rights as a research participant in this study:

If you have questions about being involved in this research, you may contact the UFIRB Office, [address & phone number]

Agreement:

I have read this re-consent form. I voluntarily agree to answer the questions for this study and I have received a copy of this form.

Participant: _____ Date: _____

Principal Investigator/Researcher: _____ Date: _____

INFORMED CONSENT FORM
FOR YOUTH INTERVIEW

South Oxnard Challenge Project

1. Purpose of the Study

RAND, a non-profit research institution in Santa Monica, California, is conducting a study to evaluate the South Oxnard Challenge Project (SOCP). The California Board of Corrections has provided funding to the Ventura County Corrections Services/Probation Agency (CSA) to implement and evaluate SOCP. SOCP offers a wider range of services than traditional probation to help youth who are on probation deal with common concerns like relationships, school performance, alcohol and drug use, mental health, and the juvenile justice system.

2. How We Selected You

We are asking you to be one of the 500 subjects in this study because you are eligible for SOCP and have been randomly assigned to SOCP or routine juvenile probation. This means you will be assigned to SOCP or routine probation purely by chance, and neither CSA nor you can pick which type of probation you will receive. Subjects will be recruited for the study during 1998 and 1999.

3. What We Will Ask You to Do

Participation in the study includes three interviews lasting two to three hours each. The first interview will occur soon after your probation assignment. The second interview will be six months after the first interview. The third interview will be twelve months after the first interview. The interviews cover:

- education and work experience
- family background
- peer relationships
- use of alcohol, drugs, and medications
- drug abuse treatment experience
- mental health treatment experience
- criminal/delinquent acts
- juvenile justice system experience
- community concerns
- friends or relatives who can help locate you for the second and third interviews

Study staff will combine information you give us in the interview, for research purposes only, with information in records about you provided to us by the South Oxnard Challenge Project (SOCP), CSA (probation department), and the police department. These records may include information about probation, arrests, and convictions, as well as information about you (such as your treatment, counseling, or training) that SOCP or CSA has received from other organizations. We will also obtain information directly from the organizations/individuals described in item 11 below, if your parent/guardian consents.

4. Payment

As reimbursement for your time and expenses, you will receive $15 for each interview, and a travel reimbursement of $10 for each interview. You may decide to get out of the study at any time. If you decide to stop participating during an interview, you will receive $5 for each half-hour of the interview.

5. Risks of Participation

Your decision to participate or not in this research study will have no effect on any aspects of your probation, including your enrollment in SOCP or other programs, the types of services you receive, or the disposition of any future charges. There is a risk that you might feel anxious, embarrassed, or depressed as a result of discussing topics in the interviews. If this occurs, study staff will refer you to a licensed counselor, your case manager, or a crisis hotline.

6. Benefits of Participation

There is no direct benefit to you. The study may benefit society by analyzing the value of juvenile justice system services such as those provided in SOCP.

7. Confidentiality

We will use the information you give us for research purposes only. We will protect the confidentiality of this information, and will not disclose your identity or information that identifies you to anyone outside of the research project. We will store your answers under a code number, not your name, and store all information containing personal identifiers in locked cabinets. We will not identify you in any reports we write. We will destroy all information that identifies you at the end of the study.

The U.S. Department of Health and Human Services (DHHS) has issued a Confidentiality Certificate to this research project. Under the certificate, RAND is authorized to and will protect your identity as a research subject in this project, even if someone tries to find out who you are through any kind of court or other legal proceeding.

RAND will not reveal your identity unless you or your legally authorized representative consent in writing. If you like, you may get a copy of this certificate by calling the Principal Investigator, [phone number].

However, this promise of confidentiality does not apply to information you give us about sexual or physical abuse of a child, or to threats of future harm to others or yourself. If we witness or are given such information, we may report it to the authorities.

8. Voluntary Participation

Your participation in the study is completely voluntary. You may refuse to participate, refuse to answer any question in the interview, or stop participating at any time and for any reason, without any penalty. We may also discontinue your participation or stop the study at any time if circumstances warrant.

9. Whom to Contact

If you have any questions about the study, please contact the Principal Investigator, Susan Turner, Ph.D., [address and phone number]. Collect calls are accepted. If you have further questions, comments, or concerns about the study or the informed consent process, please contact [name], Chair, Human Subject Protection Committee, [address and phone number].

10. Assent to Participate

I have read the statement describing the study being conducted by RAND, a non-profit research organization, and I understand what it says. I agree to participate in this study under the conditions outlined above. I also acknowledge that I have received a copy of this form. I understand that as a minor I must have the written consent of my parent or legal guardian to participate in this study.

Signature_____   Date_____

Printed Name_____   Age_____

Interviewer_____

ii. Parental Consent

I have read the statement describing the study being conducted by RAND, a non-profit research organization, and I understand what it says. I consent to allow my child/ward to participate in this study under the conditions outlined above.

CHECK ONE: __ In addition, I authorize... __ However, I do not authorize... study staff to access and obtain information from records concerning my child/ward maintained by:

- my child/ward's school(s)
- service providers
- case managers
- mental health treatment staff
- drug abuse treatment staff

I also acknowledge that I have received a copy of this form.

Parent/Guardian Signature_____

EXAMPLE IRB PROTOCOL

Title of Protocol: Understanding Offending and Victimization Experiences among Offenders	
Principal Investigator: [Name here]	**University ID #:**
Degree / Title: [Degree here] **Department:** [Department here]	**Mailing Address:** [Insert mailing address] **E-mail Address & Telephone Number:** [Insert email and phone number]
Co-Investigator(s): [Name here, if applicable]	**University ID#:**
Supervisor: [Name here, if applicable]	**University ID#:**
Dates of Proposed Research: August 1, 2008 to August 31, 2009	
Source of Funding (A copy of the grant proposal must be submitted with this protocol if funding is involved): [List funding sources here] A request for funding this research is pending from [insert agencies here, if applicable]. If awarded, the principal investigator will also submit the grant proposal to the IRB.	

(continued)

(continued)

Scientific Purpose of the Study:

This research proposes to understand the offending and crime victimization experiences of jail inmates. Specifically, this investigation will examine the relationship between crime victimization, crime perpetration, and gang membership among offenders incarcerated in jail. The scientific purposes of this investigation are to determine: (1) whether gang members experience more crime victimization than non-gang members, (2) whether gang members experience more crime victimization before, after, or during gang membership, (3) the extent to which offenders (gang and non-gang members) experience specific types of crime victimization, and (4) the extent to which offenders (gang and non-gang members) engage in specific types of crime perpetration.

Findings from this study may have important policy implications. Based on the findings of this study, policies and programs may be targeted to assist individuals or groups who are most at risk of gang membership or crime victimization.

Describe the Research Methodology in Nontechnical Language: *(Explain what will be done with or to the research participant.)*

The researchers will enter jails throughout the state of Florida and will ask jail inmates if they would be willing to anonymously and voluntarily participate in a survey. Permission to administer the survey has been obtained from several jails (e.g., name jails here) and permission to enter other jails is currently pending. Inmates will be assured that the research team is not associated with the jail and that their answers to survey questions will be anonymous since we will not collect identifying information (i.e., names or inmate number). Furthermore, inmates will be assured that they may decide not to participate, not to answer any questions they do not want to answer for any reason, or to withdraw from taking the survey at any time without penalty (see "Informed Consent" for more details). In order to minimize any perceptions of coercion, the researchers (not the jail staff) will directly ask inmates if they wish to participate.

Research participants will be asked to answer survey questions about their experiences with gangs, offending, and crime victimization. Participants will have the choice between completing the survey on their own or having the survey questions and response options read aloud to them by the researcher(s). In an effort to avoid identifying some inmates as functionally illiterate (which may result in negative stigmatization from correctional officers and/or inmates), the researchers will not ask participants or correctional officers about specific inmates' inability to read. Instead, the researchers will suggest to participants that the survey questions be read aloud while they respond to each question individually using a "paper and pencil" format. Participants will, however, have the option to complete the survey at their own pace. Given that some participants will complete the survey on their own and others will follow along as the survey is read to them, participants will begin and end the survey at different times. After participants complete the survey, they will be asked to return the surveys and the pencils. If arrangements to relocate inmates to locations within the jail are made, this will be coordinated with jail staff prior to beginning the research (e.g., participants may be moved from their cells to another room). These arrangements will also include relocating inmates who wish to discontinue participation or who finish early so that they will be able to leave the room (e.g., and be escorted by jail staff back to their cells). In some cases, the researcher may read a survey to individuals separately, should that be most appropriate for the particular jail circumstances (e.g., there is no large room to gather subjects, someone wants to participate but cannot be in the group due to other commitments such as a job assignment). Participants will be spaced adequately to make sure they do not look at others' answers. Protection procedures designed to safeguard the researchers from inmates will vary with each jail's standard procedures. For example, some jails may provide the researchers with electronic radios whereas other jails may house the researchers and participants in a room with windows near jail staff. Protection procedures will be arranged with each jail prior to and upon entry (before data collection).

The surveys will remain in the researchers' possession at all times during data collection and the jail staff will not have access to the surveys. Although surveys do not have directly identifying information (i.e., name or inmate number), the surveys will remain in the researcher's locked office. Furthermore, the dataset containing survey information will also remain in a locked office on a password-protected computer.

Describe Potential Benefits and Anticipated Risks: (*If risk of physical, psychological, or economic harm may be involved, describe the steps taken to protect participant.*)

There are no direct benefits for completing the survey for participants. By answering the survey questions, participants who have experienced past or are experiencing current crime victimization may become upset or distressed because of the nature of the questions. To minimize this potential risk, respondents will be instructed to skip any questions that they do not want to answer or to discontinue their participation in the research at any time without penalty.

Although there are no direct benefits for survey participants, there may be benefits from this research for future jail inmates and for victims of crime generally. Potential policy implications designed to assist crime victims (both inside and outside of jail) may be one future benefit.

Describe How Participant(s) Will Be Recruited, the Number and Age of the Participants, and Proposed Compensation:

Participants will be recruited from county jails throughout the state of Florida. In order to minimize any perceptions of coercion from jail staff, the researchers (not the jail staff) will directly ask inmates if they wish to participate. A convenience sample of available inmates on the days of survey distribution will be recruited to participate. The anticipated number of participants is no more than 7,000 who are at least 18 years of age. Participants will not be compensated for their participation in the research.

Describe the Informed Consent Process. Include a Copy of the Informed Consent Document:

Participants will follow along as the researcher reads the consent form (please see attached, "Informed Consent") if they wish to participate. Given that many inmates may be illiterate, the researchers will read the Informed Consent form aloud, which will help ensure the inmates (both literate and illiterate) understand the research and their rights.

As outlined in the Informed Consent, participants will be invited to participate voluntarily and will be assured that they may decline to participate, may skip any questions they do not want to answer, and may stop participating at any time without penalty from the researchers or from the jail. Participants will be told that their answers will be anonymous, given that the researchers will not know who they are (e.g., their names or inmate identification numbers will not be collected). Additionally, participants will be told that they will receive no benefits from participating, from the researchers or from the jail, and they will also be informed that there are minimal risks to participating—one of which may be remembering being victimized by crime.

Consent forms will not be collected, which will help ensure anonymity of the inmates who participate. By completing and turning in the survey, participants will be providing their implied consent for research participation. It was determined that participants may feel more comfortable answering the survey questions if they were not required to turn in a consent form that had their name/signature on it.

Principal Investigator(s) Signature:	Supervisor Signature:
Department Chair/Center Director Signature:	Date:

APPLICATION FOR A RESEARCH ASSISTANT POSITION

Professor [NAME]
Department [?]

I am looking for [**INDICATE NUMBER**] of research assistants [**INDICATE SEMESTER(S)/QUARTERS**] who would be willing to help me [**DO WHAT?**] that I am conducting with [**WHOM?**] regarding [**WHAT?**]. For this particular project, I am asking students to [**DO WHAT?**] I am looking for people who are conscientious, smart, dedicated, and interested in improving their research skills. Because this is detailed work, it is important that the research assistants be detail oriented and methodical about their work on this project. Students will need to meet with me regularly during the semester. If you're interested in gaining experience with this research project, please complete this form.

Once you submit your application, we will contact you if we are interested in interviewing you for the position. Please return completed applications to [**WHOM AND HOW?**]

Name: _____

Current Class Standing: _____ Current GPA: _____

Major(s): _____ Minor(s): _____

Mailing Address: _____

Telephone Number: _____ E-mail: _____

Please check next to the semester(s) you are applying for:

[LIST SEMESTERS OR QUARTERS HERE]

Would you be willing to be an assistant for multiple semesters?

How many credit hours are you interested in taking?
(Note: 1 credit = 3-4 hours of scheduled time/week during the entire semester)

Classes you have taken with [**PROFESSOR NAME**]:

Class: _____ Semester: _____ Grade: _____

Class: _____ Semester: _____ Grade: _____

Have you taken a research methods class? _____ If yes, what was your grade?_____

Have you taken a statistics class? _____ If yes, what was your grade? _____

Have you taken other relevant courses? Please report the course title(s) and grade(s):

To the best of your knowledge, please indicate your availability below:
Fall/Spring:

Period/Time	Monday	Tuesday	Wednesday	Thursday	Friday
[List university class times in this column]					

Summer:

Period/Time	Monday	Tuesday	Wednesday	Thursday	Friday
[List university class times in this column]					

1) Why do you want to do research? What personal skills and knowledge do you have that would make you a good contributor to our research team?

2) What are your future plans (i.e., graduate school, law school, future career aspirations)? How does contributing to research fit into those plans?

This form is adapted from one originally designed by Professor Lora Levett at the University of Florida (llevett@ufl.edu).

REFERENCES

Adams W., J. Samuels J., B. Parthasarathy, and K. Kane. 2008. Federal Justice Statistics, 2008– Statistical Tables. Table 7.11. Federal Justice Statistics Program. Retrieved from http://www.bjs.gov/index .cfm?ty=pbdetailandiid=1745.

Alderson, P. 2007. "Competent Children? Minors' Consent to Health Care Treatment and Research." *Social Science and Medicine* 65: 2272–83.

Association of State Correctional Administrators, Corrections Program Office, Bureau of Justice Statistics, National Institute of Justice. 1998. *State and Federal Corrections Information Systems: An Inventory of Data Elements and an Assessment of Reporting Capabilities.* Washington, DC: Bureau of Justice Statistics, U.S. Department of Justice.

Baltodano, H.M., P.J. Harris, and R.B. Rutherford. 2005. "Academic Achievement in Juvenile Corrections: Examining the Impact of Age, Ethnicity, and Disability." *Education and Treatment of Children* 28: 361–79.

Boruch, R.F. 1997. *Randomized Experiments for Planning and Evaluation: A Practical Guide.* Thousand Oaks, CA: Sage.

Bronson, J., E.A. Carson, and M. Noonan. 2015. *Veterans in Prison and Jail, 2011–12.* Washington, DC: Bureau of Justice Statistics.

Bureau of Justice Statistics. 2001. *Summary of Human Subjects Protection Issues Related to Large Sample Surveys.* www.bjs.gov/content/pub/pdf/shspirls.pdf

California Department of Corrections and Rehabilitation. n.d. "Visiting a Friend or Loved One in Prison." Retrieved from http://www.cdcr.ca.gov/visitors/docs/inmatevisitingguidelines.pdf.

Chaiken, J. M., M. R. Chaiken, and J. E. Peterson. 1982. *Varieties of Criminal Behavior.* NCJ 085966. Santa Monica, CA: Rand Corporation. Retrieved from https://www.rand.org/content/dam/rand/pubs/reports/2007/R2814.pdf.

Coley, Richard J., and Paul E. Barton. 2006. "Locked Up and Locked Out: An Educational Perspective on the U.S. Prison Population." Educational Testing Services. Retrieved from http://www.ets.org/Media/Research/pdf/PIC-LOCKEDUP.pdf.

Cook, C. L., and J. Lane. 2012. "Examining Differences in Attitudes about Sexual Victimization among a Sample of Jail Officers: The Importance of Officer Gender and Perceived Inmate Characteristics." *Criminal Justice Review* 37: 191–213.

Cox, D. R. 1972. "Regression Models and Life-Tables." *Journal of the Royal Statistical Society, Series B* 34: 187–220.

Coyne, I. 2010. "Research with Children and Young People: The Issue of Parental (Proxy) Consent." *Children and Society* 24: 227–37.

Davis, L. M., R. Bozick, J. L. Steele, J. Saunders, and J. N. V. Miles. 2013. *Evaluating the Effectiveness of Correctional Education: A Meta-Analysis of Programs That Provide Education to Incarcerated Adults.* Santa Monica, CA: RAND Corporation.

Davis, L. M., J. L. Steele, R. Bozick, M. V. Williams, S. Turner, J. N. V. Miles, J. Saunders, and P. S. Steinberg. 2014. *How Effective Is Correctional Education, and Where Do We Go from Here? The Results of a Comprehensive Evaluation.* Santa Monica, CA: RAND Corporation.

Davis, R. E., M. P. Couper, N. K. Janz, C. H. Caldwell, and K. Resnicow. 2010. "Interviewer Effects in Public Health Surveys." *Health Education Research* 25(1): 14–26.

Dillman, D. A., J. D. Smyth, and L. M. Christian. 2014. *Internet, Mail, and Mixed-Mode Surveys: The Tailored Design.* Hoboken, NJ: Wiley.

Erickson, D.J., and R. Tewksbury. 2000. "The Gentlemen in the Club: A Typology of Strip Club Patrons." *Deviant Behavior* 21: 271–93.

Fain, T., S. Turner, and S.M. Greathouse. 2015. *Los Angeles County Juvenile Justice Crime Prevention Act: Fiscal Year 2013–2014 Report.* Santa Monica, CA: RAND Corporation.

Farrington, D.P. 2003. "A Short History of Randomized Experiments in Criminology: A Meager Feast." *Evaluation Review* 27: 218–27.

Foley, R. 2001. "Academic Characteristics of Incarcerated Youth and Correctional Educational Programs: A Literature Review." *Journal of Emotional and Behavioral Disorders* 9: 248–59.

Fox, K.A., K. Zambrana, and J. Lane. 2011. "Getting In (and Staying In) When Everyone Else Wants to Get Out: 10 Lessons Learned from Conducting Research with Inmates." *Journal of Criminal Justice Education* 22: 304–27.

Garcia, C.A. 2016. "Developing and Maintaining Relationships with Justice Practitioners and Policy Makers." *Criminologist* 41(6): 30–33.

Goffman, E. 1961. *Asylums: Essays on the Social Situation of Mental Patients and Other Inmates.* New York: Anchor.

Goode, E. 1996a. "Gender and Courtship Entitlement: Responses to Personal Ads." *Sex Roles* 34: 141–69.

Goode, E. 1996b. "The Ethics of Deception in Social Science Research: A Case Study." *Qualitative Sociology* 19: 11–33.

Grasmick, H.G., C.R. Tittle, R.J. Bursick Jr., and B.J. Arneklev. 1993. "Testing the Core Empirical Implications of Gottfredson and Hirschi's General Theory of Crime." *Journal of Research in Crime and Delinquency* 30: 5–29.

Greenberg, E., E. Dunleavy, M. Kutner, and S. White. 2007. *Literacy Behind Bars: Results from the 2003 National Assessment of Adult Literacy Prison Survey.* Washington, DC: National Center for Education Statistics, U.S. Department of Education

Greenwood, P.W., with A. Abrahamse. 1982. *Selective Incapacitation.* R-2815-NIJ. Santa Monica, CA: Rand Corporation.

Greenwood, P.W., and S. Turner. 1993. "Evaluation of the Paint Creek Youth Center: A Residential Program for Serious Delinquents." *Criminology* 31: 263–79.

Hall, E. A., R. Zuniga, J. Cartier, M. D. Anglin, B. Danila, R. Ryan, and K. Mantius. 2003. *Staying in Touch: A Fieldwork Manual of Tracking Procedures for Locating Substance Abusers in Follow-up Studies.* Los Angeles: UCLA Integrated Substance Abuse Programs. Retrieved from http://www.uclaisap.org/trackingmanual/manual.html.

Harlow, C. W. 2003. *Education and Correctional Populations.* Washington, DC: Bureau of Justice Statistics.

Hein, I. M., P. W. Troost, R. Lindeboom, M. A. Benninga, C. M. Zwaan, J. B. van Goudoever, and R. J. L. Lindauer. 2014. "Accuracy of the MacArthur Competence Assessment Tool for Clinical Research (MacCAT-CR) for Measuring Children's Competence to Consent to Clinical Research." *JAMA Pediatrics* 168/72: 1147–53.

Hepburn, J. 2013. "Get Dirty: Keynote Address at the Western Society of Criminology Annual Conference. Berkeley, California." *Western Criminology Review* 14: 1–5.

Herberman, E. J., and T. P. Bonczar. 2014. *Probation and Parole in the United States, 2013.* NCJ 248029. Washington, DC: Bureau of Justice Statistics.

Hockenberry, S., M. Sickmund, and A. Sladky. 2015. *Juvenile Residential Facility Census, 2012: Selected Findings.* NCJ 247207. Washington, DC: U.S. Department of Justice, Office of Juvenile Justice and Delinquency Prevention.

Irwin, J. 2005. *The Warehouse Prison: Disposal of the New Dangerous Class.* Los Angeles: Roxbury.

Kaeble, D., L. Glaze, A. Tsoutis, and T. Minton. 2015. *Correctional Populations in the United States, 2014.* NCJ 249513. Washington DC: U.S. Department of Justice, Bureau of Justice Assistance.

Kimme, D. A., G. M. Bowker, and R. G. Deichman. 2011. *Jail Design Guide.* Washington, DC: U.S. Department of Justice, National Institute of Corrections. Retrieved from https://s3.amazonaws.com/static.nicic.gov/Library/024806.pdf.

Krueger, R. A., and M. A. Casey. 2014. *Focus Groups: A Practical Guide for Applied Research.* Thousand Oaks, CA: Sage.

Kubrin, C. E., and E. Stewart. 2006. "Predicting Who Reoffends: The Neglected Role of Neighborhood Context in Recidivism Studies." *Criminology* 44: 165–97.

Lambert, E. G., K. M. Reynolds, E. A. Paoline III, and R. C. Watkins. 2004 "The Effects of Occupational Stressors on Jail Staff Job Satisfaction." *Journal of Crime and Justice* 27: 1–32.

Lane, Jodi, Lonn Lanza-Kaduce, Ronald L. Akers, and Carrie Cook. 2009. *Final Report of the Florida Faith and Community-Based Delinquency Treatment Initiative (FCBDTI) Evaluation.* Submitted to the Office of Juvenile Justice and Delinquency Prevention and the Florida Department of Juvenile Justice. September, revised February 2010.

Lane, J., N. E. Rader, B. Henson, B. S. Fisher, and D. May. 2014. *Fear of Crime in the United States: Causes, Consequences, and Contradictions.* Durham, NC: Carolina Academic Press.

Lane, J., S. Turner, T. Fain, and A. Sehgal. 2005. "Evaluating an Experimental Intensive Juvenile Probation Program: Supervision and Official Outcomes." *Crime and Delinquency* 51: 26–52.

Lane, J., S. Turner, and C. Flores. 2004. "Researcher-Practitioner Collaboration in Community Corrections: Overcoming Hurdles for Successful Partnerships." *Criminal Justice Review* 29(1): 97–114.

MacKenzie, D. L. 2000. "Evidence-based Corrections: Identifying What Works." *Crime and Delinquency* 46: 457–71.

Maltz, M. D. 1984. *Recidivism.* Orlando, FL: Academic Press.

Miller, V. A., D. Drotar, and E. Kodish. 2004. "Children's Competence for Assent and Consent: A Review of Empirical Findings." *Ethics and Behavior* 14(3): 255–95.

Minton, T. D. 2011. *Jails in Indian Country, 2011.* NCJ 238978. Washington, DC: U.S. Department of Justice. Bureau of Justice Statistics.

Minton, T. D., S. Ginder, S. M. Brumbaugh, H. Smiley-McDonald, and H. Rohloff. 2015. *Census of Jails: Population Changes, 1999–2013.* NCJ 248627. Washington, DC: U.S. Department of Justice. Bureau of Justice Statistics.

Murphy, A., and S. Turner. 2009. "Parole Violation Decision-Making Instrument (PVDMI) Process Evaluation." Working Paper. Irvine, CA: Center for Evidence-Based Corrections, University of California, Irvine.

National Institutes of Health. 2011a. "Certificates of Confidentiality: Background Information." Retrieved from http://grants.nih.gov /grants/policy/coc/background.htm.

National Institutes of Health. Office of Extramural Research. 2011b. "Research Involving Vulnerable Populations." Retrieved from https://humansubjects.nih.gov/children4.

Newman, D.J. 1958. "Research Interviewing in Prison." *Journal of Criminal Law, Criminology, and Police Science* 49: 127.

Nyden, P., and W. Wiewel. 1992. "Collaborative Research: Harnessing the Tensions between Researchers and Practitioners." *American Sociologist* 23: 43–55.

Office of Justice Programs. 2016. "OJP Strategic Plan: FY 2016–FY 2018." Retrieved from https://ojp.gov/newsroom/pdfs/OJP2016 StrategicPlan.pdf.

Office of Juvenile Justice and Delinquency Prevention (OJJDP). 2016. "Statistical Briefing Book." Retrieved from http://www.ojjdp.gov /ojstatbb/.

Peak, K.J. 2016. *Justice Administration: Police, Courts, and Corrections Management.* Hoboken, NJ: Pearson.

Petersilia, J. 2003. *When Prisoners Come Home: Parole and Prisoner Reentry.* Oxford: Oxford University Press.

Petersilia, J., and S.F. Turner. 1993. "Intensive Probation and Parole Supervision: Research Findings and Policy Implications." In *Crime and Justice: A Review of Research,* edited by M. Tonry. Chicago: University of Chicago Press.

Prison Policy Initiative. 2016. "Mass Incarceration: The Whole Pie 2016." Retrieved from http://www.prisonpolicy.org/reports/pie2016 .html.

Raudenbush, S.W., and A.S. Bryk. 2002. *Hierarchical Linear Models: Applications and Data Analysis Methods.* Thousand Oaks, CA: Sage.

Riger, S. 2001. "Working Together: Challenges in Collaborative Research." In *Collaborative Research: University and Community Partnership,* edited by M. Sullivan and J.G. Kelly, 45–60. Washington, DC: American Public Health Association.

Roberts, L., and D. Indermaur. 2008. "The Ethics of Research with Prisoners." *Current Issues in Criminal Justice* 19(3): 309–26.

Roman, J. 2013. "Cost-Benefit Analysis of Criminal Justice Reforms." *National Institute of Justice Journal* 272: 30–39.

Ross, J. I., and S. C. Richards. 2002. *Behind Bars: Surviving in Prison.* Indianapolis, IN: Alpha Books.

Rossi, P. H., M. W. Lipsey, and H. E. Freeman. 2004. *Evaluation: A Systematic Approach.* Thousand Oaks, CA: Sage.

Scarce, R. 2005. *Contempt of Court: A Scholar's Battle for Free Speech from Behind Bars.* Walnut Creek, CA: AltaMira.

Sickmund, M., and C. Puzzanchera, eds. 2014. *Juvenile Offenders and Victims: 2014 National Report.* Pittsburgh, PA: National Center for Juvenile Justice.

Spence, J. T., and C. E. Buckner. 2000. "Instrumental and Expressive Traits, Trait Sterotypes, and Sexist Attitudes." *Psychology of Women Quarterly* 24: 44–53.

Steiner, B., and J. Wooldredge. 2015. "Individual and Environmental Sources of Work Stress among Prison Officers." *Criminal Justice and Behavior* 42: 800–818.

Stephan, J. 2008. *Census of State and Federal Correctional Facilities, 2005.* Washington, DC: Bureau of Justice Statistics, National Prisoner Statistics Program.

Stone, T. H. 2004. *Prisoners as Human Subjects: Researcher Reference Guide.* Louisville, KY: T. H. Stone.

Tims, F. M., and C. G. Leukfield. 1992. "The Challenge of Drug Abuse Treatment in Prisons and Jails." In *Drug Abuse Treatment in Prisons and Jails*, edited by C. G. Leukefeld and F. M. Tims, 1–8. NIDA Research Monograph Series 118. Rockville, MD: National Institute on Drug Abuse. Retrieved from https://archives.drugabuse.gov /pdf/monographs/118.pdf.

Toch, H. 1975. *Men in Crisis: Human Breakdowns in Prison.* Chicago: Aldine Transaction.

Trulson, C. R., J. W. Marquart, and J. L. Mullings. 2004. "Breaking In: Gaining Entry to Prisons and Other Hard-to-Access Criminal Justice Organizations." *Journal of Criminal Justice Education* 15: 451–78.

Turner, S., H. Braithwaite, L. Kearney, A. Murphy, and D. Haerle. 2012. "Evaluation of the California Parole Violation Decision-Making Instrument (PVDMI)." *Journal of Crime and Justice* 35(2): 269–95.

United Nations Office on Drugs and Crime. 2009. *Handbook on Prisoners with Special Needs*. Retrieved from https://www.unodc.org/pdf /criminal_justice/Handbook_on_Prisoners_with_Special_Needs .pdf.

U.S. Department of Health and Human Services. n.d. "Human Subjects Research." Retrieved from http://www.hhs.gov/ohrp /humansubjects/.

U.S. Department of Health and Human Services. 1979. *The Belmont Report*. Retrieved from http://www.hhs.gov/ohrp/humansubjects /guidance/belmont.html.

U.S. Department of Health and Human Services, Office for Human Research Protections. 2003. "OHRP Guidance on the Involvement of Prisoners in Research." Retrieved from http://www.hhs.gov /ohrp/policy/prisoner.html.

Willis, J., and A. Todorov. 2006. "First Impressions: Making Up Your Mind After a 100-ms Exposure to a Face." *Psychological Science* 17: 592–98.

World Health Organization. 2016. "Process of Translation and Adaption of Instruments." Retrieved from http://www.who.int/substance_ abuse/research_tools/translation/en/.

RECOMMENDED FURTHER READING

Decker, S., and D. Pyrooz. 2015. "'I'm Down for a Jihad:' How 100 Years of Gang Research Can Inform the Study of Terrorism, Radicalization, and Extremism." *Perspectives on Terrorism* 9: 104–12.

Gadd, D., S. Karstedt, and S.F. Messner. 2012. *The Sage Handbook of Criminological Research Methods.* Thousand Oaks, CA: Sage.

Gilmore, R.W. 2007. *Golden Gulag: Prisons, Surplus, Crisis, and Opposition in Globalizing California.* Berkeley: University of California Press.

Irwin, J. 1987. *The Felon.* Berkeley: University of California Press.

Irwin, J. 2013. *The Jail: Managing the Underclass in American Society.* Berkeley: University of California Press.

Jeffords, C.R. 2007. "Gaining Approval from a Juvenile Correctional Agency to Conduct External Research." *Youth Violence and Juvenile Justice* 5: 88–99.

Lane, J., and S. Turner. 1999. "Interagency Collaboration in Juvenile Justice: Learning from Experience." *Federal Probation* 63: 33–39.

Lane, J., and L. Lanza-Kaduce. 2007. "Before You Open the Doors: Ten Lessons from Florida's Faith and Community-Based Delinquency Treatment Initiative." *Evaluation Review* 31: 121–52.

Lane, J., S. Turner, and C. Flores. 2004. "Researcher-Practitioner Collaboration in Corrections: Overcoming Hurdles for Successful Partnerships." *Criminal Justice Review* 29: 97–114.

Latessa, E. J, S. Listwan, and D. Koetzle. 2013. *What Works (and Doesn't) in Reducing Recidivism.* Cincinnati: Anderson.

Latessa, E.J., and A. Holsinger, eds. 2015. *Correctional Contexts.* 6th edition. New York: Oxford University Press.

Lerner, J. A. 2003. *You Got Nothing Coming: Notes from a Prison Fish.* New York: Broadway Books.

Mackenzie, D. L. 2006. *What Works in Corrections: Reducing the Criminal Activities of Offenders and Delinquents.* New York: Cambridge University Press.

Maltz, M. D., and S. K. Rice. 2015. *Envisioning Criminology.* Cham, Switzerland: Springer.

Martone, C. 2005. *Loving Through Bars: Children with Parents in Prison.* Santa Monica, CA: Santa Monica Press.

Maruna, S. 2001. *Making Good: How Ex-Convicts Reform and Rebuild Their Lives.* Washington, DC: American Psychological Association.

Megargee, E. I. 1995. "Assessment Research in Correctional Settings: Methodological Issues and Practical Problems." *Psychological Assessment* 7: 359–66.

Newman, D.J. 1958. "Research Interviewing in Prison." *Journal of Criminal Law and Criminology* 49: 127–32. http://scholarlycommons.law.northwestern.edu/cgi/viewcontent.cgi?article=4691&context=jclc

Peat, B. 2011. *Case Studies in Corrections: Examples, Exercises, Discussion Points, and Practitioner Interviews.* Durham, NC: Carolina Academic Press.

Petersilia, J. 1998. *Community Corrections: Probation, Parole, and Intermediate Sanctions.* Oxford: Oxford University Press.

Petersilia, J. 2003. *When Prisoners Come Home: Parole and Prisoner Reentry.* New York: Oxford University Press.

Petersilia, J., and K. R. Reitz. 2012. *Oxford Handbook of Sentencing and Corrections.* Oxford: Oxford University Press.

Petersilia, J., and R. Rosenfeld. 2007. *Parole, Desistance from Crime, and Community Integration.* Washington DC: National Academic Press.

Petersilia, J. 1989. "Implementing Randomized Experiments: Lessons from BJA's Intensive Supervision Project." *Evaluation Review* 13: 435–58.

Stone, T.H. 2004. "Prisoners as Human Subjects: Researcher Reference Guide."

Sykes, G.M. 1958/2007. *The Society of Captives: A Study of a Maximum-Security Prison.* Princeton, NJ: Princeton University Press.

Taxman, F.S., and S. Belenko. 2012. *Implementing Evidence-Based Practices in Community Corrections and Addiction Treatment.* New York: Springer.

Trulson, C., and J. Marquart. 2009. *First Available Cell: Desegregation of the Texas Prison System.* Austin: University of Texas Press.

Welch, M. 2015. *Escape to Prison: Penal Tourism and the Pull of Punishment.* Berkeley: University of California Press.

INDEX